Sandra Watt

D0530559

Lapis Series and editing: Lapis
Graphics: RAN computer graphics and Lapis

Lapis, via Francesco Ferrara, 50 - 00191 Roma
tel/fax +39.06.3295935 e-mail: parisia@mclink.it
RAN computergrafica e-mail: ran@mail.nexus.it

Research, scientific consultation and texts: Elisabetta Pasqualin
Text adaptation: Rosaria Punzi
Paging: Maria Carrara

Translated by Isobel Butters Caleffi

© 1999 Lapis and Fratelli Palombi Editori

All rights reserved

ISBN 88-7621-923-4

Printed in June 1999 at Arti Grafiche Fratelli Palombi
Via dei Gracchi, 183 - 00192 Rome

Elisabetta Pasqualin

V ENICE
FOR KIDS

Illustrated by Lorenzo Terranera

INDEX

EQUIPMENT FOR TOURISTS

A back pack with:

- snack
- something to drink out of
- something light and water
  proof (in winter)
- hat (in summer)
- notebook
- pen
- camera with a film
- tickets for the vaporetto
- this guide

HOW TO USE THIS GUIDE

Chronological table

1300

1400

1500

On page 10 you will find a chronological table to help you find your way through the various historical periods. The different colour scale shows the earliest periods in purple which, as the years go by, turns to red. You won't find the exact dates but you will get an idea of the succession of events and the duration of each historical period.

The maps

At the beginning of each itinerary there is a general map of the area of your walk. To make it easier to know where you are and in which direction to go, each page has a detail of the main map that shows the road you are in.

The routes are in a box with a coloured background and a sign like this. Always read the information while looking at the map at the beginning of the itinerary.

Symbols

 Nearest Vaporetto stop

 The text tells a story

 The text describes the exterior of a building

 The text describes the interior of a building

Dates

Generally, when we talk of the centuries we use Roman numerals. For example you may find written: XII century, which reads: twelfth century and refers to the period from the year 1100 to 1199. In fact, the first century after Christ goes from 0 to 99, the second from 100 to 199 and so on. The dates you see in brackets after the name of an artist or important person indicate the years in which they were born and died.

On your trips around the city always try to find out something new and interesting.

Get together with a friend. The trip will be more fun and you will be able to talk about what you see together.

The museums and important buildings in Venice are often crowded, so if you don't want to spend a long time in a queue, go at opening time. The best time of year for visiting is between November and February, the worst during Carnival.

Take notes and photos; don't just take pictures of the buildings but of your friend too. It will be more fun when you look at them later.

If you really must feed the pigeons, don't let them land on you. They are greedy and very rude.

If you happen to be in Venice when it is flooded, get a pair of rubber boots at once and mind where you walk!

1500 a.C.	Neolithic people drain the marshy areas of the Veneto
400 a.C.	The area is inhabited by small communities of farmers and fishermen.
	Cleonimus of Sparta's expedition to the lagoon
0 a.C	Roman dominion
400 d.C.	
	Legendary founding of Venice
	Barbarian invasions: movement of refugees towards the lagoon
500 d.C.	Fall of the Western Roman Empire
	Venice is ruled by Ravenna
	Lombard invasion: refugees from the surrounding areas settle on the islands in the lagoon
600 d.C.	
	The bishop of Altino founds the cathedral of Torcello with a group of refugees
700 d.C.	Election of the first doge, a Byzantine magistrate
	Election of the first doge chosen from among the local families
	Increase in salt trade exchanges
	The ducal seat is moved to the lagoon
800 d.C.	Dominion of the Franks
	The doge moves to Rivo Alto
	Building of the first Ducal palace begins
	The body of St. Mark arrives in Venice. Proclamation of religious and political independence of the islands: the winged lion becomes symbol of the new state
900 d.C.	

1000	Victory of doge Pietro Orseolo against pirates: feast of the Sensa is introduced.
	Venice becomes a powerful trading centre
	Gradual conquering of the western Mediterranean territories: the Serenissima Republic is born.
1100	Venice's political influence grows
1200	
	IV crusade, conquest of Constantinople.
	Dispute with Genoa, introduction of a system of oligarchy
1300	Marco Polo's journey to the East
	The plague
	Serious external threats
1400	Peace of Turin and end of dispute with Genoa
	Cyprus is ceded to Venice
	Start of the Turkish advance
1500	
	Fight against the Cambrai league and Turks
	Neutrality towards the other Italian and European states
	Venice is one of the greatest cultural centres in Europe
1600	Victory at Lepanto against the Turks
	Crises in the Republic: plague, loss of trade monopolies, economic slump
	Start of Venice's decline: institutional crisis
1700	
	End of the Venetian Republic
1800	Napoleonic invasion. Venice is under Austrian rule
	Economic decline
	Austrian government
	Venice becomes part of the kingdom of Italy
1900	

Zones
Since 1170 the city has been divided into six zones: San Marco, Castello, Cannaregio, Dorsoduro, San Polo and Santa Croce.

Calle
Is the street you normally walk along; if it is narrow it may be called callesela or calletta, while if it is wide it is called calle larga. Once they were not paved.

Ramo
Is a short, secondary calle, often with no exit.

Campo
is the name for all the squares (except for San Marco), which once were made of earth and covered with grass (campo means field).

Campiello
Is a small campo, a small square.

Corte
Is a public space shared by several buildings.

Salizada
Was the name given to an important street, paved with blocks of trachyte volcanic rock.

Piscina
Was an area surrounded by buildings where once there was water, now filled in.

Fondamenta
Are the areas that run alongside the canals, where you can walk.

Sotoportego
(beneath the portico) is a covered passage with buildings above it.

Riva
Are places (where you can walk) that run alongside the Grand Canal in particular, or the lagoon; once ships and big boats moored along the rive.

Canal
Is a large and important waterway.

Rio terà
Was once a canal that has now been filled in. Now it's a street.

Rio
Is a small canal.

Pozzo

Is the visible part of a cistern for collecting rain water (and drinking water). They are found in the middle of a campo or a corte. Water passed through several stones with holes in them into a cistern, then it was filtered to remove the sand and it dropped into the well from which it was drawn and used. There was lots of water in Venice, but it was salty.

Bricole

Are large poles sunk in the water, sometimes found grouped together; they show the way for the boats to go and are used for mooring.

Traghetto

Is a trip from one side to the other of the Grand Canal, in gondola or vaporetto.

Palina

Is a single pole, sunk in the water and used for mooring boats. Sometimes they are striped, with the colours of the family they belong to.

Gondola

Is a typical Venetian boat; nowadays it is used to transport tourists or as a traghetto to either side of the Grand Canal. Once it was the most common means of transport, even outside the city. It has been black since 1562. Originally the felze (outer coverings) were often richly decorated. It is 11 metres long, made up of 280 different pieces of wood and is painted with seven layers of black paint. It can be rowed by single gondolier with a just one oar.

Public transports

Is usually by vaporetto or motor boat. They take different routes though. The vaporettas, larger and slower, travel right along the Grand Canal, stopping at all the stops (Line 1); the motor boats are smaller and faster and are very useful if you are in a hurry!

1. Piazza San Marco	11. Riva degli Schiavoni
2a. Procuratie Vecchie	12. Campo di San Zaccaria
2b. Procuratie Nuove	13. Church of San Zaccaria
3. Clock tower	14. Church of San Giorgio dei Greci
4. Basilica of St. Mark	
5. The bell tower and the Loggetta	15. Church of San Giorgio degli Schiavoni
6. Palazzo Ducale	16. Church of the Pietà
7. Small square	
8. Bookshop	
9. The Mint	
10. Bridge of Sighs	

St. Mark and Riva degli Schiavoni

Basilica of St. Mark (tel. 2750462)
10.00 am–5.30 pm, Sunday 3.00 pm–5.30 pm.
Bell tower (tel. 5224064) 9.30 am– 4.15 pm.
Palazzo Ducale (tel. 5224951)
9.00 am–5.00 pm, ticket office closes 3.30 pm.
Church of San Zaccaria (tel. 5221257)
10.00 am–12 pm / 4 pm–6 pm.
Church of San Giorgio dei Greci
9.00–3.30 pm, closed Tuesdays and Sundays.
Church of San Giorgio degli Schiavoni
(tel. 5228828) weekdays 10 am–12.30
am/3.00 pm–6.00 pm,
Sundays 10.00 am–12.30 am.
Church of the Pietà (tel. 52204431)
9.30 am–12.30 am / 3.00 pm–6.00 pm.

Length of visit from St. Mark to the Bridge of Sighs: half a day
from San Zaccaria to the church of the Pietà: 2 hours

San Marco Giardinetti
San Zaccaria Jolanda

PIAZZA SAN MARCO

All the squares in Venice are called "campi" except the most important of all, Piazza San Marco.

This square was the centre of political life and all the buildings that surround it were connected to the government of the Serenissima. It was here that all the most important feasts, celebrations and games in the city took place. In the IX century the doge decided to move his residence here and he had a kind of castle built, the Palazzo Ducale. In those days the square was much smaller than it is now. In the centre there was a canal, the Batario rio, beyond which there was an orchard ("brolo"), with vines and fruit trees. Where the clock tower stands now there was a sambuca tree, which the merchants used for tying up their horses.

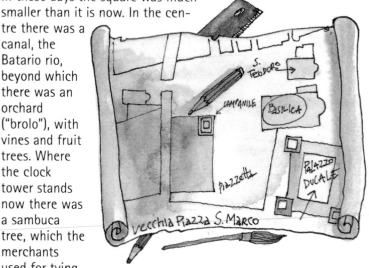

There was a bell tower too, but it was about half the size of the present one and it was mostly used as a watch tower.

The water of the lagoon went around the doge's palace-cum-castle, beside the bell tower and as far as a small church, which was the doge's private chapel. Over the centuries the square changed. Artist Gentile Bellini (1429-1507) painted a picture of the procession that took place in the square on 25 April (St. Mark's feast day) 1496. It is like a photograph of the past. The Palazzo Ducale had by then lost its fortress look. The best defence of the city was the lagoon, which separated it from the enemy like a wall.

Compare Gentile Bellini's painting with the square as it is today. Mark each element with a Y if it already existed and with a N if it was added later:

1. Clock tower with the two moors	Y	N
2. The two lions in the square to the left of the basilica	Y	N
3. The gold decoration that covers the basilica	Y	N
4. The white building behind the lions (palace of the Patriarcato)	Y	N
5. The church of San Basso near the lions	Y	N
6. The loggia at the foot of the bell tower	Y	N
7. The Procuratie to the left of the square	Y	N
8. The gold decoration on the door of the carta (the entrance to the Palazzo Ducale)	Y	N

At the centre of the square nowadays there are three tall flagpoles that were the masts of old ships.

PROCURATIE VECCHIE

With your back to the basilica, you can see the Procuratie Vecchie along the right hand side of the square.

The procuratie was the home of the procurators, the nine most important magistrates in the city, after the doge. After his investiture ceremony each procurator distributed bread to the poor, wine to the gondoliers then, after swearing his loyalty in the basilica, received an apartment in the procuratie to which his name was then given. Despite this honour, not all high magistrates were happy to leave their splendid palaces to move here. The Procuratie Vecchie were built between 1513 and 1532 following a fire that destroyed the previous ones which dated back to the XII century.

PROCURATIE NUOVE

The Procuratie Nuove are on the left hand side of the square.

They were built at the end of the XVI century by Vincenzio Scamozzi (1552-1616) and were completed in the following century.
They became the Royal Palace under the rule of Napoleon.

THE CAFES

The first coffee shop opened at the end of the XVII century beneath the Procuratie. Before long these places became very fashionable and by the XVIII century there were 24 in Piazza San Marco alone! Everyone went to them. You could gamble, make contacts, talk about business, literature or art, or simply chat. Still today there are famous old cafés beneath the arches.

CLOCK TOWER

The clock tower is to the left of the basilica beyond the small piazza dei Leoncini which takes its name from the two small red marble lions. It is built above a passageway with a vaulted ceiling. The Mercerie, one of Venice's most important shopping streets, starts here.

The clock was made at the end of the XV century.

Its face is very large and is decorated in gold and blue enamel. It has hours, signs of the zodiac and phases of the moon because:
1. it was consulted before any important decision was taken
2. it was designed to inform sailors of the tides and the best months for sailing
3. Venetians could never remember what day it was!

In a niche at the top there is a statue of Mary with Child. During Ascension week, when the clock strikes the hour, one of the small side doors opens and the angel and the Magi walk in procession past Mary, they bow and go back in through the other small door.
At the top of the tower on a small terrace are two very big statues called the "Moors" because of their dark skin. They strike the hour on a large bell. Venice was so proud of this exceptional and unique clock that the two clock makers who built it were blinded so that they wouldn't make another one like it anywhere else.
Cross under the sottoportico towards the Mercerie. Look on your left for a relief of an old lady. It is called the "vecchia del morter", the old lady with a mortar. The story goes that in 1310 a certain Baiadamonte Tiepolo devised a plot to storm the Palazzo Ducale. The

plan failed though because while the conspirators were heading towards the palace, an old lady looked out of the window to see what the noise was and knocked the mortar she kept on the sill out of the window. It fell on the head of one of the men and killed him. The Republic made this relief of her as a sign of gratitude.

BASILICA OF ST. MARK

*Go back into the
square and stop in
front of the basilica*

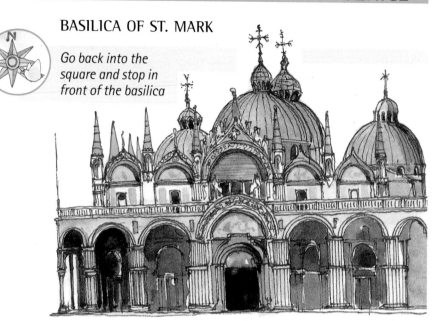

Once, the patron saint of the city was St. Theodore, but in 828 the body of St. Mark was brought to Venice. St. Mark was martyred at Alexandria in Egypt and two Venetian merchants, Buono and Rustico, decided to steal the body of the saint and bring it to Venice.

Now, how do you go about stealing a saint's body? The pair had a wonderful idea. Egyptians are Muslims and their religion forbids them from eating

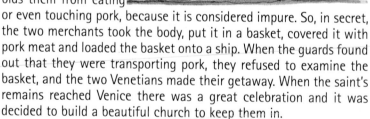

or even touching pork, because it is considered impure. So, in secret, the two merchants took the body, put it in a basket, covered it with pork meat and loaded the basket onto a ship. When the guards found out that they were transporting pork, they refused to examine the basket, and the two Venetians made their getaway. When the saint's remains reached Venice there was a great celebration and it was decided to build a beautiful church to keep them in.

Look for the different moments of the story in the mosaics in the four arches on the façade of the basilica.

The church of St. Mark was terminated in 832 but in 976 there was a revolt against the doge and the Palazzo Ducale was burnt down. The flames reached the church and it was reduced to ashes. St. Mark's was rebuilt, but again its life was short. Venice was becoming ever richer and more powerful and the church that symbolised the city needed to be a large and magnificent building.

A third building was started and this was completed in 1071. The new basilica resembled the Eastern churches. It was low and rather stocky with brick walls and low domes. Over the years it was greatly altered. The walls were covered in marble, the domes raised, and added everywhere were columns, capitals, aedicules, pinnacles, bas-reliefs and different kinds of decoration, often with an Eastern flavour. The result was a spectacular mixture of styles and elements that blended perfectly together.

The five entrance doors have large sculpted arches.
Go to the central door. The first arch contains figures with various meanings, the second shows the months of the year and signs of the zodiac and the third, the outermost one, shows the primary jobs in Venice. Try to find: the shoe menders (calegheri), the carpenters (marangoni) and the bricklayers (mureri).

Look for this strange figure with crutches biting his finger/thumb at the base of the large outer arch (on the left) of the central door. Who is it?
1. A church goer that didn't notice the steps going into the church and broke a leg.
2. The architect of the church, who is lame because such genius must be paid for by a physical defect. He is biting his finger because the church is not as magnificent as he had hoped.
3. A person pretending to be lame who has been found out and is fleeing.

At the top, in the loggia above the door are four gilt bronze horses. These are copies because the originals are in the museum inside the church. They were brought to Venice from Constantinople in 1204 by doge Enrico Dandolo (1192-1205) as booty after the IVth crusade.

Now go into the atrium and look up. This is just the beginning of a huge open Bible, an infinite stretch of gold and over 4.000 square metres of mosaics.

Once most of the population could not read and the simplest way of teaching them the stories of the Old and New Testaments was to show them in pictures. The mosaics in the atrium tell stories from the Old Testament.

Look for the Creation of the World and the Great Deluge.

Why did they use mosaic? The pieces are made of glass (which has always been worked in Venice) and their reflection creates a special light, bright, warm and diffused in all directions. They also serve to form a golden cloak that hides the brick walls.

If you touch part of a mosaic you soon find out that it is not smooth. Each piece is inserted at a different angle so that the surface of each piece reflects light in a different direction, otherwise it would seem like a mirror.

If you wish, you can go up to the horses' gallery. You will see the basilica gleaming in a gold light and you will be able to admire the original four horses close up, go out to the loggia, walk on the roof of the basilica and see Piazza San Marco from high up.

It's an amazing experience!

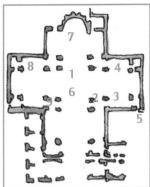

Go into the church (there is a set route and you are not allowed to stop for very long). The plan is a Greek cross — with four equal arms — covered by five domes. It was modelled on the church of the Twelve Apostles at Constantinople, which no longer exists nowadays. In front of the main altar is the **iconostasis (1)**, a screen dividing the presbytery (the area reserved for the clergy) from the rest of the church, a common feature in Eastern churches. On the screen are statues of the Madonna, St. John the Baptist and the twelve Apostles.

On the **right pilaster (2)**, on the side towards the entrance, there is a relief of the Madonna, known as the Madonna of the Kiss because it was so highly venerated that it was kissed and touched by everyone.

Go into the right arm, beyond the columns, and look for a mosaic that tells the story of the **finding of St. Mark's body (3)**. The adventures of the saint did not end when his body arrived in Venice. During the restoration work that took place in 1063 his body was hidden in the church for fear that it might be stolen. Unfortunately, it was so well hidden that nobody was able to find it again. The story goes that the people of Venice prayed, special services were held, fasts were organised, but all were in vain. The body of St. Mark had vanished without a trace. Thirty years passed. Finally St. Mark, tired of being hidden, decided to let himself be found: he stuck his arm out of the pilaster in which he had been hidden, spoiling the marble decorations in the meantime. It was 25 June 1094. He was taken to the crypt to be buried, and great celebrations followed. However, in the XVI century the crypt was closed because it was always flooded with water and the saint's body was forgotten again! It was not found this time until 1811 when it was placed beneath the main altar, where it still is now. The first scene of the mosaic shows everyone praying, while in the second the miracle is taking place. St. Mark reveals the place in which he has been hiding. Can you see where in one of the columns a window opens and an arm is coming out?

To find the **pilaster of the miracle (4)**, turn your back to the mosaic and face the small altar in front of you to the left, up against a pilaster. The right wall of the pilaster is the site you are looking for. It is marked by a cross in relief.

Now you can go and see the **treasure of St. Mark (5)**, items of antiquity and religious pictures brought from Constantinople. One of the corner towers of the old Palazzo Ducale was situated in this area.

On your way back go and look at the **great dome (6)** in the centre of the church. The mosaic decoration (XIII century) represents Jesus rising to Heaven, the moment known as the Ascension. The "feast of the Sensa", which takes place every year to celebrate the event, is one of the most important occasions in Venice.

Beneath the great dome is a kind of sea — a stretch of floor made of strips of light coloured marble. The veining resembles the waves of the sea.

Go and see the **Gold Altarpiece (7)** behind the main altar. It is one of the most valuable objects in the world! Entirely made of gold, it is composed of 250 painted pictures, enamels and 3.000 precious stones. Doge Pietro Orseolo (976-78) ordered it from Constantinople in 976. The roundels in the border belong to this early phase. Over the centuries other parts have been added: the stories of the Gospel and St. Mark (in 1105) and the stories of the life of Christ (1209). The silver frame is Gothic and belongs to 1345, like the central roundel with Christ, the Evangelists and twelve Apostles.

The altarpiece itself is supported on a pivoting device. On special occasions it is turned towards the altar so that the congregation can admire it.

Beneath the main altar is the body of St. Mark. Notice the **four columns** that support the canopy above the altar. These are made of alabaster, belong to the V century and are decorated with scenes from the Gospel. There is nowhere in the basilica that is not decorated, not even the smallest place!

Beneath this area known as the presbytery is **the crypt** (XI century), where you can go if you get permission. It is very impressive. The vaults are supported by low columns. In the centre is the altar and, behind, a large rock. It was here that St. Mark's body was found in 1811, over seven hundred years after it had been solemnly laid there in 1094.

Go and see the **altar (8)** on the right. On it is an old picture (XII century) of Mary with Jesus in her arms. It came from Costantinople in 1204 and is called the Nicopeia, which means "bringer of victory" in Greek. It has always been considered the protector of Venice and once was used in battle as the symbol of the Byzantine army. It is still much venerated today.

Look at the floor, it seems like a huge carpet. 1.500 square metres of mosaic! There are geometric designs, birds and other animals, each with its own symbolic meaning.

After the Nicopeia altar look at the beginning of the left aisle for an old relief (XIII century) of the **Madonna of the rifle (9)**. Right next to it is a rifle left by a sailor who was miraculously unhurt when an ammunitions deposit exploded during the 1848 war.

Look now at the decorations on the walls. The designs are formed by the veining in the large slabs of marble cut, opened like a book, and then placed side by side.

Leave the basilica and look for:

a. the tetrarchs, the four emperors who shared the empire at the time of Diocletian (IV century A.D.).
According to legend they are the four "moors",

turned into statues because they tried to steal the treasure of St. Mark's

b. the Madonna of the little baker; so-called in memory of the "poor baker of Venice". In 1507 Pietro Faziol, a young baker, was hanged between the columns of the square, wrongly accused of murder. Shortly afterwards the real murderer confessed and the magistrates, in a belated attempt to redress the balance, placed candles around the picture of Mary in memory of the unfortunate man. Look for it high up

c. two tall pilasters that come from St. John's at Acri in Syria. They were brought here following the victory by the Venetians in 1256 over the Genoese, who at the time occupied Syria

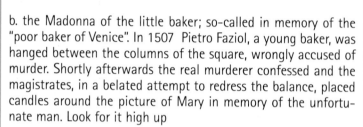

d. the proclamation stone. State proclamations and laws were publicly read simultaneously from this porphyry column and another one at the Rialto. In so doing they became legally binding.

In 1902 the bell tower collapsed suddenly and it was this stone that bore much of the impact, sparing the basilica from damage.

THE BELL TOWER AND THE LOGGETTA

The bell tower, fondly known as the "paròn di casa" (man of the house, the host) was built in the XVI century. It is almost 100 metres high and, although it does not seem so, the brick part makes up half the entire tower.

At the top is a gold angel which shows the way the wind is blowing when it moves. The bell tower has always provided a reference point for sailors. The very first construction dates back to 888; then it was solid and built like a turret. The roof was covered with mirrored slabs which shone in the sun so that they would be visible from a long way away (now the angel performs the same function). At night, wood was burned in the belfry for the same reason. In the following centuries the tower was raised, rebuilt and altered. Suddenly on 14 July 1902 it fell down. The proclamation stone saved it from falling towards the basilica, which was completely undamaged and no one was hurt. It was rebuilt exactly the same and in the same place, "as it was, where it was". There are five bells which each had a specific role. The biggest, the Marangona (from the word marangon, meaning carpenter) announced the beginning and end of the working day, while the smallest, the Maleficio (the evil one) announced capital punishments.

Go to the top of the bell tower and you will be rewarded with a magnificent view! It was from here that in 1609 Galileo showed doge Leonardo Donà how his telescope worked. In those days the only way up was on foot. At the base of the tower is the Loggetta (small loggia); it was built in the XVI century by architect Jacopo Sansovino (1486-1570). From here the Arsenalotti, the doge's loyal followers, kept the peace during the sittings of the Great Council which took place at the Palazzo Ducale.

PALAZZO DUCALE

In 810 doge Agnello Partecipazio (804-11) decided to move the seat of the government here and, on his own land, built a large fortified palace with corner towers, a moat around it and drawbridges.

After various fires, in 1340 building began on the palace you now see (25.50 metres tall). The Palazzo Ducale was the home of the doge, but it was also the centre of political life in the city.

This palace is an exceptional example of Gothic art and it was built in a rather special way. Usually the fullest and "heaviest" part of a building is at the bottom, while the upper floors have more windows; here the opposite is true.

On the ground floor there is a portico, on the first floor, open loggias and the top floor is one long wall.

The main entrance to the palace was by the "porta della Carta".

The name "porta della Carta" (door of Paper) derives from:

1. the State archives that were near here

2. the fact that the scribes, who wrote letters for illiterate people, were to be found here

3. the decoration which was so fine and delicate it seemed like paper lace

The door was made between 1438 and 1442 by Bartolomeo Bon, a famous Venetian artist. Originally it was painted in light blue and gold. At the top there is a relief of Francesco Foscari (1423-57), who was doge at the time the door was made. He is shown kneeling before the lion of St. Mark. Above is a bust of the saint and at the top Justice holding the sword and scales.

The long loggia on the first floor is broken up by Gothic arches. All the columns have differently decorated capitals and sculptures in the corners.

Look for these two details on the columns

If you look at the large balcony where the loggia facing the jetty is, you will see the **Wheat door**. Its name comes from the nearby "Corn office" which dealt with the ordering of wheat supplies.

Go into the palace. Immediately to the left is the Museo dell'Opera. Carry on and beyond the ticket office you will find yourself in the inner courtyard of the palace.

It is part of one of the most famous buildings in the world, seat of the city government, palace of justice and residence of the doge.

The four sides of the courtyard were not all built in the same period, and in fact are rather different from one another.

On the last Sunday of Carnival a bull hunt used to be held here to amuse the doge's maidservants.

The staircase of the Giants

If you turn right you will come to the **staircase of the Giants (8)**, built at the end of the XV century by Antonio Rizzo (1430-99). It was at the top that the doge was crowned. The youngest among those that had elected him placed a white cap called the "camauro di rensa" on his head. Then also on his head the eldest placed the "zogia", the ducal hat decorated with 66 precious stones and symbol of power.

Go back in the direction of the Censori staircase, go up to the Loggia and turn right. You will come to the Golden staircase (1). It belongs to the middle of the XVI century and takes its name from the wealth of white and gold decorations in the vault. Either side you will see two large statues: Hercules killing the Hydra (a mythological monster, here used to symbolise the Turks) and Atlas holding up the world.

When you get to the first landing turn right and go up the stairs to the **doge's apartment (2)**.

Have you noticed that the rooms are bare and empty? When the doge was elected he brought his furniture with him, and when he died the apartment had to be cleared in the following three days.

First floor

The doge (from the Latin dux, commander) was elected for life by the older members of the most prominent Venetian families. He represented the Republic, but could not take any decisions alone. As a result he had six advisors who were always with him in meetings, or when he travelled outside the city.

The first room you come to is known as the **Scarlatti room (3)**, perhaps because of the scarlet red togas worn by the noblemen who made up the ducal procession and who awaited the doge here.

In the **Grimani room (4)**, which takes its name from the doge depicted in the gold coat of arms on the ceiling, there is a painting by Vittore Carpaccio (1460-1526). It shows the lion of St. Mark, symbol of the city, with its front paws on the ground and its back ones in the water to indicate that Venice's power reached over land and water.

Walk along until you get to the **Philosophers' room (5)**, which takes its name from the personages once portrayed on the walls. Behind the door on the right is a staircase leading to the upper floors. Go up six steps, then stop, turn round and look at the wall above the door. The large fresco you see was painted in 1523 by Titian (1490-1576). It shows St. Christopher crossing a river and carrying baby Jesus on his shoulder. It is said to bring luck.

Whoever looks at it will have good luck all that day! From here go across the **Map room (6)**, the **Equerries' room (7)**, and then head for the **Golden staircase (8)** landing. Go up another floor.

You are now at the **square Atrium (9)**. In many of the episodes represented on the walls you will find a doge. It was a good way of having your portrait painted so that you were not forgotten! The octagonal painting on the ceiling, by Jacopo Tintoretto (1518-94), doge Girolamo Priuli (1559-67) is represented as a personification of the city to whom Justice hands the sword. Watching the scene are Peace, St. Mark and the Lion.

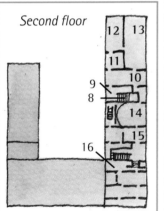

Second floor

From the Atrium go into the room of the **Four Doors (10)**, which is as big as the whole palace. On one side the windows overlook the rio di Canonica and on the other, the inner courtyard.

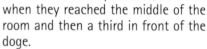

This was where ambassadors and important figures waited to be received by the doge, so it is hardly by chance that the decorations exalt the power and greatness of Venice.

Look for a painting by Tiepolo (1696-1770) in which Neptune offers the riches of the sea to Venice. The city is represented by a beautiful woman cloaked in the royal fur ermine and holding the crown and sceptre. Beside her is not a little dog but a lion!

Carry on until you reach the **room of the Anticollegio (11)**. This was the antechamber for foreign ambassadors. Now go through to the **room of the Collegio (12)** where the "Pien Collegio" met. This was formed by the Signoria, or rather the doge, the six councillors and the three heads of the Quarantia. The Pien Collegio met every day except for Sundays and Mondays.
The job of the Signoria was to prepare bills to be presented to the Senate.
When the ambassadors were admitted to the room they had to make a first bow as soon as they went in, a second when they reached the middle of the room and then a third in front of the doge.

The decorations on the walls celebrate the greatness of Venice. The paintings on the ceiling are by Paolo Veronese (1528-88). In the oval near the tribune, Justice and Peace offer their symbols of the sword, scales and olive branch to Venice enthroned.
Enter the **Senate room (13)**, known also as the "Begged" room, because the magistrates were "Begged" by the doge in writing to attend the sittings.

The Senate was set up in the XIII century. Initially it was composed of 60 members who increased to three hundred in the XVI century.

During meetings the doge and some of the magistrates sat on the raised wooden dais known as the tribunal, while the other senators sat along the walls.

If you continue you will return to the room of the Four Doors and this will take you to the **Council of Ten room (14)**.
Despite its name, the council was actually made up of 17 people, ten magistrates, the doge and his six councillors.
The magistracy was introduced in 1310 after Bajamonte Tieplo and his plotters' attempt to overturn the government failed. They were discovered by the doge and stopped as they were heading for the Palazzo Ducale (you can read this story on page 19).
It was the duty of the Council of Ten to condemn conspirators and prevent future attacks. It became a sort of secret police with the right to spy on whoever was suspected of plotting against the republic.
This room was known as the "cheba", the cage, because the meetings were top secret.
The room leads directly to the **Compass room (15)** where suspects awaited questioning by the Council of Ten.

Go towards the exit. On the right there is a sort of double wooden door in the wall. Go out and see what is on the other side. It is the mouth of a lion with just the outline left.
What was it for?
1. To report crimes against the state?

2. To hear what was said in the room?

3. It was a kind of lie detector. Prisoners put their hand in it and if it came out unscathed they were telling the truth!

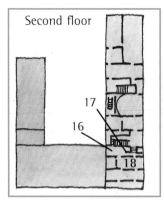

Second floor

You are at the **Censori staircase**. Go up two flights of stairs and you will reach the Council of Ten's **room of the Arms (16)**. So as to be always ready, the republic decided in the XVI century to keep a deposit of weapons inside the palace. Part of these were lost when the republic fell.

First you will come to the **room of Gattamelata (17)**, a famous condottiere who fought for the republic between 1433 and 1442, the year in which he died. The armour you see on the right behind glass is his.
Look between the doors for the armour of Henri IV of France, who gave it to Venice personally in 1604.

First floor

The following room is dedicated to **Morosini (18)**, a great Venetian admiral whobecame doge after conquering the Peloponnese in the XVII century. You can see his bust among the many swords, halberds, crossbows, shields and helmets.

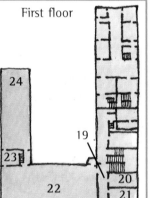

Return to the landing of the **Censori staircase**, go down two flights and turn left. Now you are in the Liagò (19), the passageway leading to the Maggior Consiglio. Here the noblemen met during breaks in the Council meetings.

Walk right along the Liagò, passing the **Quarantia Civil Vecchia room (20)** and **Armament room (21)** where once weapons and ammunition were kept. It was connected to the armoury above it by means of a staircase.

At the end of the Liagò on the right is a door leading to the **room of the Maggior Consiglio (22)**, the body that approved laws and elected the doge and most important magistrates. All noblemen over the age of 25 could belong to the Maggior Consiglio.

Council meetings were held on Sundays and they were announced by the ringing of the bell of San Marco. They were strictly private and it was forbidden to participate armed.

Apart from the most important magistrates, who sat on the tribune, the others sat back to back on chairs laid out all down the room.

It was also here that the first steps towards electing a doge were taken. It was a complicated procedure, with secret votes and lot drawing to avoid cheating.

In 1577, a terrible fire broke out near here and it destroyed the room completely. When it was restored a frieze of all the doges was painted along the upper parts of the walls.

Look for a black flag in the place of one of the pictures. It covers the portrait of Marin Faliero (1354-55), the doge that was decapitated for allegedly plotting against the state.

Behind the tribunal is the largest painting on canvas in the world. It is 7 metres high and 24 metres wide. The subject is Paradise and it was painted in 1592 by Jacopo and Domenico Tintoretto to replace a painting of the same subject that had been destroyed in the fire.

On the ceiling is the glorification of Venice. Here too the city is shown as a beautiful woman.

Look for the oval near the tribune where Paolo Veronese (1528-88) painted "the triumph of Venice". Seated among the clouds, the personification of the city is about to receive the royal crown. Now look at the panel in the centre. It is the work of Jacopo Tintoretto (1518-94) and shows doge Nicolò da Ponte offering Venice the gift of the cities under its rule.

What does Venice give to the doge in return?

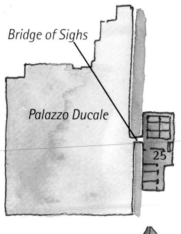

The door on the right at the end of the room leads to the **Quarantia Civil Nuova room (23)** and from there you get to the **Ballot room (24)** where votes for the election of the doge and other magistrates were counted.

The frieze with portraits of the doges continues in this room too, ending with Ludovico Manin (1789-97).

On the right wall is the large painting of the battle of Lepanto (1571). The whole decoration of the room in fact recalls naval battles fought in the East by the Venetians.

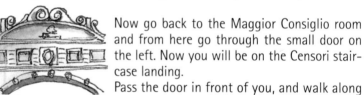

Look for commander Sebastiano Venier. He has got white hair, is wearing armour and is standing on a red ship with many oars.

Now go back to the Maggior Consiglio room and from here go through the small door on the left. Now you will be on the Censori staircase landing.

Pass the door in front of you, and walk along until you get to a steep staircase. You are about to walk along the same passages, staircases and dark, low corridors that the many condemned men had to cross to reach their cells. These will bring you to the building of the **New Prisons (25)**.

Bridge of Sighs

You will also cross the **bridge of Sighs**, the internal link between the Palazzo Ducale and the New Prisons, terminated at the beginning of the XVII century.

Palazzo Ducale

25

On your way you will pass several small cells with heavy iron bars, low wooden doors, sturdy locks and no light, where the prisoners spent their time in punishment.

Another staircase will take you back across the bridge of Sighs, which is divided into two corridors. From the small square windows you can see the Canonica bridge on one side and on the other the dock of St. Mark and island of San Giorgio.

There were dark and gloomy prisons in the palace itself too. These were known as the "wells" because they were so damp and were often literally under water. The cells just beneath the roof instead were called the "leads".

Once you are back in the Palazzo Ducale, cross the rooms whose names derive from the different government associations that used to meet in them such as the **room of the Censori,** who checked that the elections were carried out correctly and that nobody rigged them. The **room of the Avogaria,** or State lawyers, a magistracy that dates back to the XII century and other rooms, until you are back in the open gallery.

Turn right along the gallery and go to the **Senators' staircase** that will take you down into the **Senators' courtyard.**

Its name may originate from the custom of the magistrates to pause here to talk before going into the palace.

Go to the **Foscari arch,** a covered passageway with pinnacles, spires and statues on the outside.

From here, go through the porta della Carta and you will be back in the square.

THE PIAZZETTA

The piazzetta is the area that goes from the basilica to the dock of St. Mark, between the Palazzo Ducale and the Library.

Once it was a wet dock, a small port where ships were moored. In the XII century it was filled in to prevent the waters lapping the basilica and bell tower. Two columns brought from the East in 1172 were placed near the water's edge; the first is that of St. Mark with the lion on top, while the other is that of Tòdaro (St. Theodore) who is shown killing a dragon (Theodore was a warrior saint which is why he is shown defeating a monster).

Once the columns, very close to the water, marked the ceremonial entrance to the city (the only way to reach Venice was by sea). It is said to be unlucky to walk between them because it was here that executions once took place.

In actual fact there were three columns originally but, while they were being unloaded from the ship, one fell in the water and it was never recovered. Recently, divers have looked for it but without success.

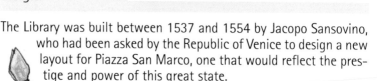

THE LIBRARY

It is on the right, looking at the isle of San Giorgio.

The Library was built between 1537 and 1554 by Jacopo Sansovino, who had been asked by the Republic of Venice to design a new layout for Piazza San Marco, one that would reflect the prestige and power of this great state.

The library was to contain documents and valuable ancient manuscripts such, for example, as those that cardinal Bessarione gave to the city in 1468. Added to these were all the books printed in Venice. In 1500 there were 493 printers and publishers in Venice!

Sansovino's design included an open gallery, like the one at the Palazzo Ducale, with a system of arches that would recall the buildings of the past.

Work began on the corner near the bell tower, for which the architect had decided on a vaulted ceiling. Suddenly though, on 18 December 1545, most of the vault collapsed and Sansovino who was held responsible went to prison. He was kept there for two years, until he had paid the sum to repair the roof out of his own pocket.

Work continued but it was terminated by another architect, Vincenzo Scamozzi (1552-1616).

THE MINT

Go past the library and turn right. The mint overlooks the dock of St. Mark. It was built by Jacopo Sansovino in around 1540.

It was here that all the gold and silver coins of the Republic were minted. The Italian word zecca meaning mint derives from the Arabic sikka, meaning money. Venetian money was accepted everywhere. One face showed the lion handing the standard of the city to the doge and the other bore the figure of Christ, whereas in other states important people were usually represented.

Why were there no portraits of famous people on Venetian coins?
1. The doge was the most important person in the city, but it was his role that was important, not the person himself.
2. The Venetians, considered extremely ugly, did not want to be portrayed.
3. Venetians did not know the art of making such small portraits.

BRIDGE OF SIGHS

After walking right to the end of the Palazzo Ducale, you get to the Paglia bridge. It is one of the oldest bridges in the entire city.

From here you can see the world famous bridge of Sighs.

Its name comes from:
1. the sighs of the courting couples who went by in a gondola beneath it
2. the sighs of the doges who, getting older all the time, had a hard time climbing all that way up
3. the sighs of the prisoners as they walked from the jail to the courtroom.

RIVA DEGLI SCHIAVONI

Go over the Paglia bridge – its name comes from the boats loaded with straw (paglia) that used to stop here until 1285. Now the Riva degli Schiavoni is in front of you.

The waterfront takes its name from the inhabitants of Schiavonia (Slavonia or Dalmatia), one of the first lands to be conquered by the Republic of Venice. The Schiavoni, who arrived in the city at the beginning of the XV century, were craftsmen, merchants and above all sailors. They moored their boats here and nearby was what is known as their scuola (school), which helped the poor but was also rather like the guilds in other parts of Europe. The Riva degli Schiavoni runs alongside the basin of St. Mark, Venice's most important stretch of water. All the doge's important visitors (emperors, princes, ambassadors) moored their ships at this quay.

CALLE DELLE RASSE

Once past the Prisons, which you see immediately after the bridge, you reach the calle degli Albanesi, from the name of another foreign community, and right after that is the calle delle Rasse.

The rassa or rascia was a large piece of wool cloth imported from the principality of Rascia in Serbia by the Schiavoni and it was sold in this area. It was used particularly for making the "felze" which covered the gondola and protected it in bad weather and allowed the passengers greater privacy. Little by little, the covered area of the gondolas increased and became more and more elaborate and by the 1700's it had come to resemble a drawing room with sofas, mirrors, lamps and windows. In 1172 doge Vitale Michieli was assassinated during a procession in front of the calle delle Rasse. In those days the Riva degli Schiavoni was very narrow and consequently ideal for ambushes, so the route of the procession was changed.

CAMPO DI SAN ZACCARIA

Continue on your way and after the next bridge go under the sottoportico on the left to campo San Zaccaria, which takes its name from the church dedicated to St. Zachary.

The whole complex – church, convent and campo – once belonged to Benedictine nuns. Each morning the gates of the campo were opened when the bells rang and were closed again at sundown.

CONVENT OF SAN ZACCARIA

Either side of the church stood the buildings of the convent of San Zaccaria. It was an extremely ancient and very important institution. The nuns that lived there were all young girls of wealthy noble families, closely connected and often related by kin to the doge and the

magistrates of the Republic. When they entered the nunnery they brought large dowries that helped to make San Zaccaria wealthy and powerful. Life in the convent however was not always austere and dedicated only to prayer.

Just think that in the XVIII century masked balls and entertainment took place in the parlour where the nuns received visits. In 864 the abbess of San Zaccaria gave doge Pietro Tradonico the first "horn", the hat decorated with 66 precious stones that later became the symbol of the doge and the Republic. In sign of his close ties with the convent, at Easter every year the doge came to visit it and received a straw hat as a gift.

In 1100 it was decided to extend St. Mark's square. The small Batario canal that ran across the middle in front of the basilica was filled in and the San Zaccaria nuns gave the doge their orchard, which extended beyond the canal.

CHURCH OF SAN ZACCARIA

In the IX century after Christ, doge Giustiniano Partecipazio founded the church of San Zaccaria here.
After the numerous additions and modifications that took place over the years, the building you see was completed in 1515.

The façade is divided vertically into three parts; the windows are high, narrow and dark, in contrast with the white of the façade. This play of colours, open and closed spaces was devised by Mauro Codussi (1440-1504), the architect that designed the church, to create a sense of movement in the façade and give it a highly individual look.

Go into the church and look around: you will see that here too the architect has alternated black and white.

Go up to the second **altar on the left (1)**. There is a large painting of the Madonna and saints. It is a work by Giovanni Bellini (1430-1516).

What device does the artist use to give the impression that the space of the painting continues that of the framework of the altar?
1. a door in the painting takes you directly into the sacristy.
2. the painting is in actual fact a chapel because you can walk behind the Madonna's throne.
3. the capitals and pilasters in the painting are the same as the stone ones of the altar.

Cross the nave and look for the **second altar on the right (2)**. Here you will find the urn containing the body of St. Zachary, father of St. John the Baptist.
Continue on the right, go through a door and into the Sant'Anastasio chapel, which leads you to that of **San Tarasio (3)**.

You are now in the apse of the older church of San Zaccaria (early XV century). The windows are tall and slender with pointed quatrefoil arches (meaning which terminate in a decoration that looks like a four-leaf clover). All this is in the Gothic style.

The ceiling is divided into segments. God is in the centre and several saints are around the sides. It was frescoed by Andrea del Castagno (1420-1457), a Tuscan artist. He painted in the Florentine manner, in the style called Renaissance, creating pictures that were faithful to reality with colours very similar to nature and above all laying emphasis on movement, volumes of the body and facial expressions.

At this time the local artists continued to paint in the Venetian style, using bright colours and gold backgrounds to create a sense of the divine, and fairytale-like figures. The **floor of the first church**, X century and decorated with a mosaic similar to that in St. Mark's basilica, was hidden beneath a later one. A few areas have been uncovered and you can see them in the areas cordoned off **(4)**.

Compare the figures on the ceiling with the three poliptyches. They date from the same period (1442/3) and yet:

1. look at the folds of the clothes; which hang more naturally?
2. which faces seems more realistic to you?
3. is the sense of depth accentuated or flattened by the gold background?

Go down the stairs beside the chapel. Now you are in the **crypt (5)** of the earlier church. It dates back to the X century and it is a small church in itself, with a low ceiling supported by two rows of columns with small denticulated capitals. Eight doges are buried here.

Once the level of the floor was not so low and it was not flooded as often as it is now. This is because the ground level in Venice is slowly sinking.

Go out and with your back to the church, go to the door at the other side of the campo; it has a bas-relief of the Madonna and St. Zachary.

The saint has a bandage round his head. Why?
1. because he was a priest
2. because he was martyred with a blow on the head
3. because he suffered from terrible headaches.

CHURCH OF SAN GIORGIO DEI GRECI

Turn right and when you get to campo San Provolo, turn right again to the fondamenta dell'Osmarin and walk right the way along it. Go over two small bridges and turn right. Soon after, beyond a large black gate on the right, you will come to the public buildings of the Greek community, the church, bell tower and school.

Foreign communities of people from areas outside the confines of the Republic were numerous in Venice; there were Albanians, Slavs, Milanese, Florentines, people from Lucca and many others. Although the Greeks had been living in the city since ancient

times, they did not receive permission to build an Orthodox church until the XV century.

Notice how crooked the bell tower is! It looks as though it is about to fall into the water. Indeed, it started to lean before it was even completed in the late XVI century. This is because the layer of land collapsed on which the foundations lie.

Go into the church and have a look around. The elaborate decorations on the walls are almost all by Greek artists. Above the entrance door is the ladies' gallery where women attended the mass, divided from the men.

Along the walls either side of the entrance there are two orders of chairs and a wooden choir where the clergy sat during the service.

Go up to the iconostastis. It is a kind of wall decorated with religious pictures, that here are painted in the Eastern manner with lots of gold, figures with dark faces, sharply defined outlines and a fixed stare. The iconostasis separates and hides the area of the main altar from the part where the congregation sits.

The only openings are the three doors. The one in the centre is called the holy door and only the priest or bishop can pass through it. It is usually found in Greek-Orthodox churches.

Leave the church and look for a well. What is shown on it?
Can you find the same scene represented at least five different times?

SCUOLA DI SAN GIORGIO DEGLI SCHIAVONI

When you leave the church go back, walk down the calle della Madonna, go past the bridge and the calle dei Greci, then go straight on. Turn left immediately after the bridge and go along the fondamenta dei Furlani. The School of the Schiavoni is at the end, at the foot of the next bridge.

It was built at the beginning of the XVI century. Look at the façade.

It is oddly unsymmetrical — the windows on the ground floor are all different.

In the past bread and a bowl of hot soup were given to the poor through the largest of the windows.

The School was partly set up to provide for those in need, the poor or homeless.

You can visit the School. The Dalmations (Schiavoni) held meetings in 1451 in a school. During these encounters, they chose as their protectors the saints of their religion, George, Tryphon and Jerome. When it was given a precious relic of St. George, they decided to embellish the building with paintings that would illustrate episodes from the lives of their three saints. They commissioned Vittore Carpaccio (1460-1526) to paint nine canvases. (You can see them around the walls above the seats). The climate in Venice is very damp

and frescoes, painted directly onto the walls, do not last long. This is why Venetian painters did not paint on the wall itself but on large canvases made of linen or hemp which were exactly the same size as the space they were to decorate.

Underline the 8 mistakes contained in this story by comparing it with what you see in the canvases.

St. Jerome, bishop of Split, retired to a monastery when still young. One day a wounded crocodile arrived, much to the terror of all the monks who fled as fast as their feet could carry them. The saint, unafraid, took the thorn out of the dog's tail and healed it. From that moment on, the lion stayed on to live in the castle as a pet. St. Jerome however was very old and soon died.

The second scene shows his funeral. It does not seem like a sad occasion though and the only detail connected to death is the skull lying on a table on the right.

The last scene shows a miracle. While St. Augustine is in his study, a divine light suddenly appears and he hears the voice of St. Jerome announcing his death. Even the parrot is struck dumb by the extraordinary event taking place!

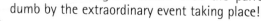

The next pictures recall episodes connected to St. George. You try to fill in the words missing in the story. George, a young ...., arrives in a part of Libya where there is a terrible and ferocious .... which exists on a daily diet of live young people. It is the king's daughter's turn to be devoured. When the saint sees the dragon, he attacks it with his .... The animal is fatally wounded and the ....saved.

The dragon is made up of parts of other animals. Which ones?

1..

2..

3..

4..

5..

The dragon is dying. St. George makes a lead with the princess' belt and takes it into the town. The royal family and all the townspeople convert to Christianity and are baptised by St. George.

The last canvas tells the story of an episode in the life of St. Tryphon, a child saint that persuaded the devil in the form of a monster called a basilisk to spare the emperor Gordian's daughter.

Find the differences between this little dragon and the one killed by St. George?

....

....

....

OSPEDALE DELLA PIETÀ

Leave the church go back across the bridge, walk along the salizarda dei Greci, then turn left into the calle dei Greci and go on down calle Bosello. Turn left at the crossroads then right into calle della Pietà.

You are walking along beside the old Ospedale della Pietà, an orphanage for abandoned babies, poor children, or orphans.

In the past, people that for one reason or another were unable to keep their children, left them at these hospitals. In moments of great financial crises they were so full of babies that a sign was put up (look for it) to discourage the practice. Parents contemplating the idea of leaving

their offspring were threatened with the most dreadful punishments in the next world.

Each hospital had a uniform. The one of the young girls at the Pietà was red.

The girls were educated and taught to play a musical instrument, and the hospitals corresponded to the music conservatoires of today.

These girls were known all over Europe and when an important person came to Venice they would hold a concert in honour of the distinquished quest.

CHURCH OF THE PIETÀ

At the end of the calle della Pietà you reach riva degli Schiavoni. The church of the Pietà overlooks it.

The church originated in the XV century but it was rebuilt in the middle of the XVIII by architect Antonio Massari (1686-1766).

The girls from the hospital held their concerts here.

Between 1703 and 1740, the choir of the Pietà was directed by Antonio Vivaldi (1678-1741), a famous composer-priest, also known as the "red priest" because of the colour of his hair. Concerts held in the church soon became one of Venice's major attractions.

Since the church was also used as a music room, the architect designed it so that the acoustics would be perfect.

If you go in you will see that it is oval and that the ceiling has no corners.

The fresco on the ceiling is by Giambattista Tiepolo (1696-1770) and it shows the "Triumph of the Virgin".

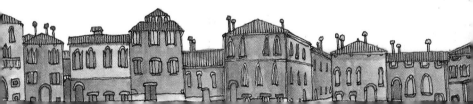

1. Rialto bridge
2. Palazzo dei Camerlenghi
3. Palazzo dei Dieci Savi alle Decime
4. Church of San Giacomo di Rialto
5. Fabbriche Nuove
6. Fondaco dei Tedeschi
7. Campo San Bartolomeo
8. Corte del Milion
9. Church of Santa Maria dei Miracoli
10. Scuola Grande di San Marco
11. Basilica of Santi Giovanni e Paolo
12. Ospedaletto dei Derelitti
13. Campo and Church of Santa Maria Formosa

The Rialto zone from the Rialto to Santa Maria Formosa

Church of Santa Maria dei Miracoli (tel. 2750462). 10.00 am-5.00 pm, Sunday 1.00 pm-5.00 pm.
Scuola Grande di San Marco (tel. 5238368) entrance at civil hospital.
Basilica of Santi Giovanni e Paolo (tel. 5200633). 8.00 am-12.30 am/3.00 pm-6.00 pm, Sunday 3.30 pm- 5.30 pm.
Church of Santa Maria Formosa (tel. 270462). 10.00 am-5.00 pm, Sunday 1.00 pm-5.00 pm.

Length of visit
Rialto Zone: 1 hour
From Rialto to Santa Formosa: 2 hours

Rialto

THE COMMERCIAL AREA OF RIALTO

As its old name Rivus Altus suggests, this is the area where the waterside is highest, providing greater safety from flooding. Not only this, but its position in the centre of the lagoon protected it from invasions from the sea.

During the XI century the commercial centre of the city grew up here. The big market you still see has been here for centuries.

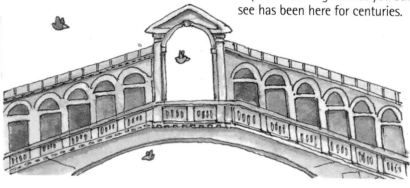

RIALTO BRIDGE

It was here that the Rialto bridge was constructed, the only connection between the two sides of the canal for hundreds of years.

In the Middle Ages the bridge was built on boats (a bit like the bridges that are erected for the feasts of the Redentore and Salute), then in the XIII century it was replaced by one made of wood. But the new structure cannot have been much more solid than the first. It was restructured a great many times over the next 200 years until 1444 when the weight of a crowd, gathered to watch the marquis of Ferrara pass by, caused it to collapse. It was built in wood again, but this time with a row of shops either side and a mobile part in the centre (like a castle drawbridge) to let the big ships carrying merchandise through.

This painting by Vittore Carpaccio (1460-1526) shows what the bridge looked like then. At last, in 1557, it was decided to build one in stone. A competition was held and many architects took part, including Andrea Palladio and Michelangelo. The winner was Antonio del Ponte, perhaps because of his name — ponte means bridge! (1512-97). His is the one you see today.

A rather strange game used to take place on the Rialto bridge — the wheelbarrow race. In 1700 two wheelbarrow pushers, Cosmo and Gasparo, dustmen by profession, had a bet as to which one could get across the bridge first, avoiding people and holes. We do not know who won but

afterwards it became a real race where the winner received a prize of wine and money.

At the Rialto the areas beside the Grand Canal take their names from the goods that were unloaded there.

Go up to the centre of the bridge and face St. Mark.
The left bank (where the Actv line 1 vaporetto stop is) is the riva del Carbon where coal was unloaded and sold and the timber merchants sold their wood.

Ca' Loredan and Ca' Farsetti, two of the oldest buildings in Venice, both overlook this area. Built in the XIII century, they are now used to house the Municipality and its offices.

Further on, near the Rialto bridge, is the riva del Ferro (Actv Stop, lines n. 82 and 52) while, on the other side of the canal, is the riva del Vin where the ships loaded with wine used to moor. Here too was the Land customs, where goods coming from the mainland were checked and weighed. Goods coming from the sea went to the Sea customs at the Salute.

THE RIALTO MARKET

Now leave the bridge and go in the direction of the riva del Vin. You will find yourself in the middle of the market.

PALAZZO DEI CAMERLENGHI

The large white building you see on the right is palazzo dei Camerlenghi, where the three magistrates lived who dealt with state finances.
On the ground floor there were three small cells where debtors or people who did not pay their taxes were kept. It was built between 1525 and 1527, in a very elegant style, right where the canal bends. Nowadays it is the Audit Office.

PALAZZO DEI DIECI SAVI ALLE DECIME

On the left is the Palazzo dei Dieci Savi alle Decime (a sort of Ministry of Finance) with a portico facing the Grand Canal.
You are in the ruga degli Oresi, the street where for centuries the goldsmiths, silk and wool merchants had their shops. Nowadays there are fruit and vegetable stalls here while the jewellers' shops are under the sottoportico on the left.

Look for this statue.
What does it represent?

1. Victory
2. Justice
3. Abundance

Look for some names of road and water ways hidden in the phrases:

1. look under the rug and...
2. call each other
3. the camp on the top of the hill

CHURCH OF SAN GIACOMO DI RIALTO

Among the flower, vegetable and fruit stalls on the right you will see the back of a small church called San Giacometto.
It is traditionally considered to be the oldest church in the city, dating back to the V century A.D., but in actual fact it was probably built in the XII century.

Look high up on the outside and you will see a XIII inscription in the shape of a cross. Just below that is another sign warning merchants to be honest, precise in weighing their goods and to respect their contracts.

When you look at this church carefully you will see that there are some rather odd things about it – the small terrace of a nearby house is almost touching the bell tower, for example! You will find the oddest thing though by walking round the church. It is a huge clock in the middle of the façade. There was already a clock in the Middle Ages. It must have been very important to know the time (nobody had wristwatches then) in such a busy place. Over the centuries the church of San Giacomo was home to a number of schools connected to the activities that took place in the area. The goldsmiths, exchange merchants and cheese sellers had altars here, as did many other merchants.

CAMPO DI SAN GIACOMO DI RIALTO

The church of San Giacometto overlooks Campo San Giacomo di Rialto. The buildings on the left and right are the Fabbriche Vecchie, rebuilt after a terrible fire that in 1514 destroyed the whole quarter. Once the porticoes on the ground floor were full of shops and workshops, while the upper floors housed public offices.

THE HUNCHBACK OF RIALTO

On the other side of the campo opposite the church is the "talking" statue of the Hunchback of the Rialto. Look for the small curved man supporting the steps up to the "Proclamation stone", a column from which laws and sentences were cried out, making them the public (there is another in St. Mark's square). He was said to play tricks on people, like the statue of a certain Pasquino in Rome. Sometimes he was even made to have conversations with Pasquino.

FABBRICHE NUOVE

The Fabbriche Nuove are on the Grand Canal on the right.
Designed by Jacopo Sansovino (1486-1570), they were once the seat of the merchants' administration. The market covers this entire area: the Erbaria, along the Grand Canal, where the fruit and vegetable boats still unload today, the Cordaria (for the cord merchants), the Casaria (where cheese was sold), campo delle Beccarie (meat sellers) and campo della Pescheria, where the fish market still is. It is the furthest away because it was the least important – fish is one thing there is no shortage of in Venice!
Finally, if you carry on you come to Riva dell'Ogio, where oil from Sicily, Puglia and Crete was unloaded. Of course there was also a sort of bank and insurance company (in calle della Sicurtà) which insured the big boats full of goods that sailed to and from Venice.

Go to ruga degli Speziali (the spice merchants' alley)

Look for the sculpted apples.

Carry on towards the bridge of the Beccarie that crosses the canal of the same name.

Look high up on the right at the roof of a house with chimney stacks in the shape of upturned bells, one of the oldest and most typical sorts of chimney in Venice.

They were also sometimes shaped like a cube, fork or trident and were often decorated like fans with flowers or small geometric patterns.

As you wander round, remember to have a look because there are still some left.

In this area of the Rialto too all the names of the calle or campo come from the activities that took place there.

Can you say which of these names have been invented?

1. calle dei Botteri (Barrel makers lane)

2. calle del Cappeller (Hat makers lane)

3. campo dei Mascherai (Mask makers square)

4. campo dei Manigoldi (Rogues' square, because of all the thefts that took place)

5. calle degli Australiani (Australians' lane, where the Australians had a school)

Now make your way back towards the Grand Canal, cross the bridge of the Due Spade, go under the sottoportico of the Due Spade and straight on to the Due Mori portico. If you turn left, then immediately right, you will be back in the ruga degli Oresi.

FONDACO DEI TEDESCHI

Go onto the Rialto bridge and stop in the middle; look out over the Grand Canal in the direction of the Ca' d'Oro. At the foot of the bridge on the canal side are two old buildings facing one another. On the left is palazzo dei Camerlenghi, on the right fondaco dei Tedeschi.

Rialto was an important place for foreign exchange. The city's foreign communities used the "fonteghi" (warehouses) for their trade practices. These buildings belonged to the Republic and were let to the merchants. Here the foreign traders talked business, stored their merchandise and even slept.

The Tedeschi (as all central European peoples were called)

were one of the richest communities and their relationship with Venice was always very close.

On the night of 27 January 1505, the fondaco dei Tedeschi was destroyed by fire. The goods that went up in smoke included rooms filled with gold, and the value of the loss was greater than that of the entire city of Antwerp, one of Europe's wealthiest cities!

It was decided to rebuild the warehouse immediately and two famous painters, Giorgione and Titian, were commissioned to decorate the exterior. Unfortunately, because the climate is so damp only fragments are left of the frescoes.

The commercial use of the warehouses was reflected in the regularity of the ground plan and distribution of the rooms. The ground floor had a portico facing on to the water so that the goods could be unloaded from the boats directly into the building where they were then stored. Also on the ground floor but on the outside there were shops facing the calle. On the upper floors there were offices and homes.

CAMPO SAN BARTOLOMEO

Leave the Rialto bridge and go to campo San Bartolomeo

In the centre of the campo there is a statue of Carlo Goldoni (1707-93), Venice's greatest playwright.

CORTE DEL MILIÒN

Leaving campo San Bartolomeo behind you, go down salizarda dei Tedeschi and carry straight on until you get to the church of San Giovanni Crisostomo. Turn right and take calle dell'Ufficio della Seta. Go under two sottoporticoes and arrive in corte (courtyard) del Miliòn.

This is where Marco Polo lived. In 1271, when he was 17, he left for the Far East with his father and uncle.

When he arrived in China he became a great friend of the leader of the Tartars. When the three returned home 24 years later, no one recognised them until they dressed as Venetians again.

When they did, they were greeted with huge celebrations. His incredible adventure is told in the Million, his book about the wonders of the world, exotic countries and people then entirely unknown.

Look on the walls of the courtyard for these shapes. What animals are they?

Marco Polo lived in the houses you can see over the sottoportico, where there are still traces of XIII century decoration, for example the windows with pointed arches and, lower down, two large sculpted arches which lead to the corte del Teatro.

CHURCH OF SANTA MARIA DEI MIRACOLI

With your back to Marco Polo's house, go under the sottoportico, at the end of which there is a bridge. From there go straight on to campo Santa Marina. Cross the campo and take the calle on the left that leads to the Cristo bridge. Immediately after, turn left along calle dei Castelli. In front of you is the church of Santa Maria dei Miracoli.

In the XV century a gentleman living near here exhibited a painting of the Madonna (which you can see on the altar inside) said to perform miracles. In 1480 the decision was made to build a church worthy of such an important picture.

Architect Pietro Lombardo (1435-1515) was chosen for the job. He liked to decorate his buildings with polychrome, or multi-coloured marble. Materials left over from the building of St. Mark's were used for this church.

Above the façade is a rounded lunette shape, rather reminiscent of a precious casket.

Go into the church. You will notice something unusual. The altar is higher up than the church, at the top of a flight of steps.

Which of these decorative elements can you see?

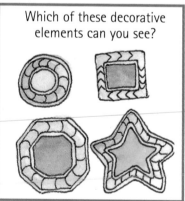

The whole church is decorated with coloured marble and when you go in you cannot help being struck by its elegance and the wealth of decoration. This church is considered one of the most beautiful in Venice and it is a very popular place to get married.

CAMPO SANTI GIOVANNI E PAOLO

Cross Santa Maria Nova bridge and turn right along fondamenta Piovan. Cross another three bridges and you will come to campo Santi Giovanni e Paolo.

This campo was very important because one of the richest churches in the city was located here. In the "campo of wonders", as the Venetians called it, feasts and ceremonies were held, and even the funerals of doges (which the people did not always attend because there was a long-standing belief that the church would fall down during a ceremony of this kind).

In the centre of the campo is an equestrian monument by Verrocchio, Leonardo da Vinci's master, of Bartolomeo Colleoni, a XV century condottiere who served the Republic. He left most of his wealth to Venice on the understanding that a statue in his honour would be erected in front of St. Mark's. Since it was out of the question (not even the doge could have a statue of himself in the square) but no one wanted to forfeit the large inheritance, the statue of Colleoni was indeed placed in front of St. Mark's – St. Mark's school though!

SCUOLA GRANDE DI SAN MARCO

The building on the left, nowadays the Civil Hospital, was once the Scuola Grande di San Marco (a kind of school). After being entirely burnt down in 1489, it was rebuilt by Pietro Lombardo (the same architect who worked on Santa Maria dei Miracoli). The interior was altered during the XIX century and little remains of the original.

You can visit the Library though, the Chapter room and the Hotel room of the old Scuola Grande. The entrance is through the hospital.

BASILICA OF SANTI GIOVANNI E PAOLO

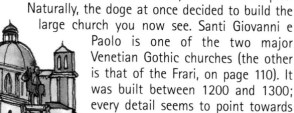

Beside the old school is the basilica of Santi Giovanni e Paolo, the largest church in Venice.
The Venetians call it San Zanipolo (from Zani = Giovanni and Polo = Paolo). There is a story that once there was just a small church here in this campo, but one night, nearly 800 years ago, the small church appeared in a dream to doge Jacopo Tiepolo surrounded by flowers, doves and angels, and a voice announced that this place had been chosen by the Lord's disciples. Naturally, the doge at once decided to build the large church you now see. Santi Giovanni e Paolo is one of the two major Venetian Gothic churches (the other is that of the Frari, on page 110). It was built between 1200 and 1300; every detail seems to point towards heaven. Notice all the elements typical to the Venetian Gothic style: the arches on the façade, the roof decorations, the very tall and narrow windows along the sides with their pointed arches and trefoil or quatrefoil decorations (like clover leaves). The façade is broken up horizontally into two parts. The lower one contains the large entrance door

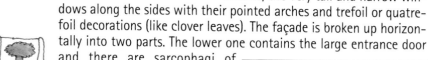

and there are sarcophagi of doges and other important figures in niches. The upper part of the façade is divided into three parts which correspond to the internal divisions.

Go in. The columns are big and very high so that the ceiling seems very far away. Numerous important people are buried here, including no less than 15 doges! Soon after the entrance on your right is the **monument to Marcantonio Bragadin** (1523-71) (1).

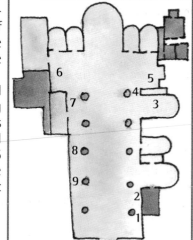

It was erected to honour the valorous commander who defended the island of Cyprus against the Turks. After ten months of siege the Venetians had to surrender (1571). Bragadin was taken prisoner and was skinned alive. The Venetians, however, stole the skin from the Turks, placed it in an urn and brought it here, where the monument was built in his memory. Can you see the urn?

On the second **altar on the right (2)** there is a poliptych (a painting made of several parts hinged together) showing Vincenzo Ferrer between St. Christopher and St. Sebastian. It was painted by Giovanni Bellini (1432-1516) a famous Renaissance artist. He used bright, luminous colours. Look how he paints the angel's feathers, they almost seem to be made of enamel!

Can you find this detail?

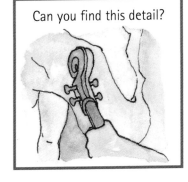

Go towards the **chapel of San Domenico (3)**, the saint who founded the Dominican order to which this church belongs. The ceiling is slightly curved to give the idea of a dome and is painted in such a way that it resembles an endless stretch of sky, into which angels and saints appear to be sucked away into a vortex. Some people are leaning out over the cornice and looking upwards. They are balancing and almost seem to be about to fall on top of us. In XVIII century painting it was fashionable to create an impression of breaking through the ceiling, and this is what Giambattista Piazzetta (1683-1754) has done here.

Right outside the chapel there is a small altar dedicated to **St. Catherine (4)**.

Look at the valuable reliquary — it contains one of the saint's feet!

Now go towards the left where there is a **huge stained glass window (5)** made by the master glass makers of Murano. They did not only make vases, plates and lamps, but also coloured sheets of glass that, placed over wooden outlines, could be cut into whatever shapes they wished.

The shading, folds of the clothes, eyes, nose and mouth were painted on the glass which was then baked.

The various coloured pieces were then put together like a large mosaic and held together with the lead that surrounded them.

On the other side of the church in front of you is the door to the **Rosary chapel (6)**. Look at the big 24 hour clock, which has been made to work again only recently. By the beginning of the XVI century wall clocks like ours were already in use in Venice. Naturally there were still sundials, which showed the time by the shadow of a pointer cast by the sun.

At the beginning of the left aisle there is a small altar with a painting of **St. Joseph holding baby Jesus (7)**. It was painted at the end of the XVI century by Bolognese artists.

Just after that, look on the wall of the aisle for **three paintings on wood (8)**. In the centre is St. Augustine and either side are St. Lawrence and St. Domenico. The background is gold and the figures facing us head on, are static, almost statue-like. They were painted in 1473 but Bartolomeo Vivarini, the artist, was still tied to the manner of the previous century.

Go towards the entrance of the church and before leaving look for the **group statue of doge Giovanni Mocenigo (9)**. The doge lies calmly between two women who represent the Virtues and he is surrounded by various other figures. Look for the three children drawn here at the side.

When you leave the church, go over to the well. It is made of Istrian stone, sculpted as though it were the capital of a column with eight children running around it.

OSPEDALETTO DEI DERELITTI

Cross the campo and head for Barbaria delle tole

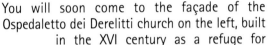

The word Barbaria was used to indicate North Africa which was where the "tole", or wooden boards, were sent that were kept in warehouses near here.

 You will soon come to the façade of the Ospedaletto dei Derelitti church on the left, built in the XVI century as a refuge for orphans, the old and the sick.

Like the Ospedale della Pietà (page 48), this one also became famous because the girls who stayed here were taught music.

 To reach the Music room where they gave concerts, you have to go up a large oval spiral stair-case that belonged to the original building.

You reach a small frescoed room. There is something odd about this room – it has got no corners!

Above the door there is a corridor where the girls would play, hidden behind a grate so they were not seen.

Why has the room got no corners?
1. to bounce balls off the walls
2. so that the acoustics are perfect
3. for dance rehearsals.

There is a grate on the opposite wall too, but this time it is false, like the space that has been created all around: a portico with six steps, the columns and capitals, even the dog, shadows included.

CORTE BOTTERA

Go back towards the campo until you get to calle Bressana then turn left and left again to fondamenta Felzi. Take a few steps up the bridge, then turn left immediately.

Now you are in the very old corte (court-yard) Bottera, where time seems to have stopped. This is where the coopers (botteri) made or mended barrels.

CAMPO AND CHURCH OF SANTA MARIA FORMOSA

From fondamenta Felzi, cross one of the two bridges and turn right at the end into calle lunga di Santa Maria Formosa. Walk right along it until you get to Santa Maria Formosa.

In the VI century the Madonna is said to have appeared in a dream to St. Magnus bishop, instructing him to build a church on the site where he saw a small white cloud. The bishop obeyed. The name Santa Maria Formosa means "shapely St. Mary" and comes from the fact that the bishop remembered a well-rounded lady appearing in his dream.

You are in one of Venice's most beautiful campi, surrounded by beautiful old buildings. Entertainment and games were once held here. The church is rather special too because it has two fronts, one on the campo and one on the canal.

Go in and visit it. Architect Mauro Codussi (1492) who designed it emphasises the interior space by alternating grey and white.

The church was the headquarters for several schools, the artillery men and the chest makers who built the wedding chests young ladies would put their worldly goods in and which served as their dowry when they married.

It is said that one day in the year 948, some Slav pirates kidnapped 12 girls at a party at San Pietro di Castello. At once the Venetians, helped by the chest makers, chased after them by boat and brought them back.

To recall the event, every year at the "festa delle Marie" on 2 February, the six zones of Venice used to collect money for a dowry to give to 12 needy girls, who then paraded past the doge along the Grand Canal as far as the church of San Pietro di Castello.

St. Barbara was protector saint of the bombardiers and she was prayed to especially before battles. Look for a painting of her in the bombardier's chapel.

What are the saint's feet resting on?
1. a cannon
2. a carpet
3. a stool

Walk around the church and look for a mask above a door. It was there to stop the devil from entering, ringing the bells and frightening the people!

If you still have time, go and see the Querini Stampaglia foundation museum, just behind the church of Santa Maria Formosa.

It is a beautiful XVIII century building with furniture and paintings of the same period.

1. Ca' d'Oro
2. Strada Nova
3. Scuola Grande di Santa Maria di Valverde
4. Campo dell'Abbazia e della Misericordia
5. Old site of Scuola Grande di Santa Maria di Valverde
6. Palazzo Mastelli or Palazzo Cammello
7. Campo dei Mori
8. Tintoretto's House
9. Church of Madonna dell'Orto
10. Campo and church of Sant'Alvise

From Ca' d'Oro to Sant'Alvise

Ca' d'Oro
(Galleria Franchetti tel. 5238790).
9.00 am-2.00 pm.

Church of Madonna dell'Orto
(tel. 2750462). 10.00 am-5.00 pm,
Sunday 1.00 pm-5.00 pm.

Church of Sant'Alvise
closed

Length of visit: 2 hours.

Ca' d'Oro

CA' D'ORO

The Ca' d'Oro overlooks the left bank of the Grand Canal.

Today it is a museum, but once it was a private house that had such sumptuously dazzling decorations of light blue, black, white and especially gold that it was called the Cà d'Oro (House of Gold).

In 1412, Marino Contarini a procurator of the Republic decided to build himself the most splendid home in Venice. He bought the land and hired the best tajapiera or stone cutters in the city to work for him. He may even have designed the building himself — whatever the case, the result was spectacular.

If you arrive by boat from the Grand Canal you can get a good view of the façade. Today, the gilding that gave the palace its name can no longer be seen but all the openings and coloured marble make the architecture light and yet rich. It is a wonderful example of flamboyant Gothic, the style popular in XV century Venice.

As in all old Venetian houses, the Ca' d'Oro has a large portico on the ground floor that reaches right up to the Grand Canal. The main route was by water and Venetians were often merchants, so their homes served as storerooms and the goods unloaded from the boats were brought across a portico such as this directly into the hall on the ground floor. From there they were taken to the deposit.

On the upper floors there are large open galleries embellished by windows with pointed arches, above which are four-lobed flowers set in rectangles.

STRADA NUOVA

After leaving the Ca' d'Oro on your left is the calle d'Oro. Go along it. At the intersection with Strada Nuova, turn left and go straight on until you get to San Felice bridge. Cross over it, turn right immediately and walk along the fondamenta until you have to turn left.

The bridge in front of you is an odd shape and has a strange name - it is called ponte Chiodo (Nail bridge). It has no parapet and very wide steps.

The old Venetian bridges that linked the small islands to the city were all like this.

Why did Venice's bridges have wide steps?
1. horses had to cross over them
2. fewer materials were used to build them
3. they were on the route of the famous bridge race.

NEW SITE OF THE SCUOLA GRANDE DI SANTA MARIA DI VAL VERDE

Turn left and walk to the Misericordia bridge. The building you see on the right is the new Scuola Grande di Santa Maria di Val Verde, sometimes called the Misericordia.

In 1534 the confraternity of the Scuola Grande di Santa Maria di Val

Verde decided that their old home (it is behind here and you will see it soon) was too small, so they sold it and called a very famous architect, Jacopo Sansovino (1486-1570) to design the new building on a site nearby that already belonged to them.

It is called Val Verde (Green Valley) because:
1. it recalls a miracle
2. there is a picture of Mary sitting in a meadow
3. it was once surrounded by meadows.

CAMPO DELL'ABBAZIA OR DELLA MISERICORDIA

Walk along the right-hand side of the School, go over a wooden bridge and you will be in campo dell'Abbazia.

As you cross the bridge try counting the steps on one side and then on the other – the number is not the same. This is because the water level is not the same for all the small islands of which Venice is made up. The paving of the campo is not made of the usual grey trachyte stone. Here a very old method has been used of arranging bricks to make a herring bone design. Once the squares of Venice were simply made of beaten earth or of bricks like this. This is one of the few left now. There is a well in the centre with two brothers of the Scuola Grande depicted on it. They are wearing the monk's habit and are holding the symbol of their brotherhood, or confraternity, the initials SMV.

SMV means:
1. Santa Maria Val Verde
2. Some Mad Venetians
3. Saintly Martyrs of Venice

OLD SITE OF THE SCUOLA GRANDE DI SANTA MARIA DI VAL VERDE

In front of the bridge you can see the church that gives this area its name. On the left, instead, is the old home of the Scuola. The church is built of brick, while the school is made of stone.

Walk through the sottoportico that goes under the Scuola Vecchia (old school) and carry on along the fondamenta. As you walk along you will come to a door with an image of the Madonna of the Misercordia (with her cloak open to receive the brethren). There were houses here that the school gave to the poorer members. When you are in the corte Vecchia, turn right and go across the bridge. On the horizon you can see the island of San Michele, Venice's cemetery.

PALAZZO MASTELLI OR PALAZZO DEL CAMMELLO

When you get off the bridge, turn left along fondamenta Gasparo Contarini (1483-1542), a distinguished cardinal and literary man who lived here at number 3539.

Continuing on the other side of the canal, there is a building with a relief of a camel. It is known as the Palazzo del Cammello (Camel building), but its real name is palazzo Mastelli, from the name of its owners.

Originally the building may have been the warehouse of the Arabs before it became the home of three brothers, Rioba, Sandi and Alfani. Some say that these three brothers — rich Arab merchants — arrived in Venice after fleeing from Morea, a region in Greece, where they had been caught up in a civil war.

In Venice they were known as "Moors".

Perhaps the brothers had the relief of a man in a turban leading a camel placed on the front of their house as a reminder of their Eastern origins.

It is said that their family name Mastelli (Tubs) refers to the many containers full of gold coins that they owned!

CAMPO DEI MORI

Go over the bridge you see on your left and you will come to campo dei Mori.

Look for the three brothers.

What is the suitcase-like object they are carrying on their shoulders?

1. the burden of their fame
2. the backpack used by the merchants of the time
3. their riches.

FONDAMENTA DEI MORI

You will find a fourth Moor, called Antonio Rioba, on the wall of the façade of Jacopo Tintoretto's house. Tintoretto was a famous Venetian painter who lived at number 3399 of the fondamenta that starts immediately to the left of the bridge at the end of the campo. The statue of Rioba was thought to be a talking statue, like the Hunchback of Rialto (page 56).

CAMPO DELLA MADONNA DELL'ORTO

Go back, cross the bridge and you will come to the campo Madonna dell'Orto.

The name derives from an old statue of Mary with Child that was said to perform miracles. It was found in an orchard nearby and was taken to the church. The campo is paved in the same way as the campo della Misericordia you saw before.

SITE OF THE ANTICA SCUOLA DEI MERCANTI

In the left corner, looking at the church, is the site of the Antica Scuola dei Mercanti (old Merchants' School). There were many merchants in this area who traded with the islands in the northern lagoon as well as with the mainland (this part of the city faces the mainland).

The patron saint of the Scuola dei Mercanti was St. Christopher (his name means "he who brings Christ"). It is said that Christopher was very big and strong and that he worked as a ferryboat man, carrying people from one side of the river to the other.

Once he carried a child on his shoulder who, as he walked in the water, gradually became heavier and heavier. It was Jesus. St. Christopher therefore became the protector of perils concerning water, and this is why the school and originally the church too, were dedicated to him.

CHURCH OF THE MADONNA DELL'ORTO

The church of the Madonna dell'Orto was built towards the end of the XIV century. It was once dedicated to St. Christopher and you can see a statue of him above the entrance door.

The brick façade is divided vertically into three parts which correspond to the three aisles inside.

Have you noticed how the white niches, statues, arches and flowers stand out against the red of the bricks?

All the details decorating the façade are typical elements of the Venetian Gothic churches: the two large side windows with pointed arches, the double rows of small white columns that separate them, the flower-like decorations with three or four petals and large "eye" (the round, or rose window).

The interior of the church is divided into three parts by Greek marble columns. The ground plan is unsymmetrical because there are chapels on one side but only altars on the other. This is because on the right the wall was up against a cloister, so it was impossible to build on that side. However, sometimes where space was missing it was created... by painting. Go up to the first altar on the right and look at the oil painting, it seems like a sort of open chapel. In the centre is St. John the Baptist with other saints either side. John's face is turned upwards towards God and he seems to be looking at the real light that enters the church through the window. Continue along the right aisle until you reach the door of the chapel of St. Maurus.

Above it is a very large painting of the **Presentation of the child Mary** (she was three years old) **at the temple.**

It is by Jacopo Tintoretto (1519-94), a famous painter who lived in this area (you saw his house earlier on) and who painted many of the paintings kept in this church.

He is also buried here. To show us who the main character of the scene is, Tintoretto uses light to create a "route" for our eye to travel along, so that we are led directly to the most important figure.

The very old statue of Mary that gave its name to the campo is kept here in the St. Maurus chapel.

In the chapel to the right of the presbytery is the tomb of Tintoretto. His will has been reproduced and copied too. He also painted the

two large canvases you see either side of the main altar (4). In the first on the left, the **Adoration of the golden calf** there are two episodes happening at the same time: in the upper part Moses (the figure with wide open arms) is receiving the tablets of the law from God and the angels, without wings here, on Mount Sinai; in the lower part the Hebrews, who wanted to create an idol, are collecting earrings and necklaces to build a golden calf.

The calf, which serves as a model, is standing amongst the jewels that the women are still collecting. Here too, Tintoretto creates areas of strong light, while leaving others in deep shade.

The large canvas on the right, by Tintoretto too, shows the **Last Judgement**. At the top Jesus is seated on the clouds; in one hand he is holding a lily, representing mercy, and in the other the sword of justice. Below, the saints and apostles are seated on the clouds then, as you get lower, there is the immense crowd of those who will be saved or condemned.

Look for these details in the two paintings and find the intruder.

A

B

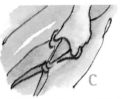
C

The paintings behind the main altar are also the work of Tintoretto.

Now turn towards the nave and look up at the galleries
One is open, while the other is closed, in fact it is fake.

Why is one of the two galleries fake?
1. there was not enough room to build a real one
2. people could spy from behind the fresco on what was going on in church
3. the real gallery was so ugly that they decided to cover it up with fake architecture.

CAMPO DI SANT'ALVISE

With your back to the church of Madonna dell'Orto, follow the fondamenta to the right, cross the wooden bridge, walk right along calle Loredan until you reach fondamenta della Sensa (Ascension).

You have to take this roundabout route to get to the island, although it is nearby, because there is no direct link.

Cross the Rosso bridge, go on a little, then turn right along calle del Caoitello. Cross another bridge and you will be in campo Sant'Alvise.

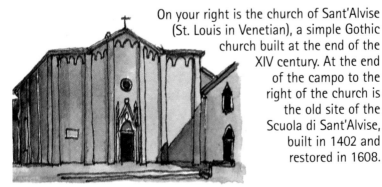

On your right is the church of Sant'Alvise (St. Louis in Venetian), a simple Gothic church built at the end of the XIV century. At the end of the campo to the right of the church is the old site of the Scuola di Sant'Alvise, built in 1402 and restored in 1608.

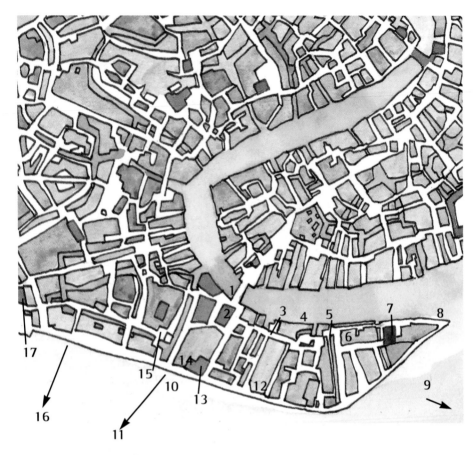

1. Campo di Santa Maria della Carità
2. Gallery of the Accademia
3. Campo San Vio
4. Palazzo Venier dei Leoni
5. Campiello Barbaro
6. Campo San Gregorio
7. Basilica of Santa Maria della Salute
8. Punta della Dogana
9. Island of San Giorgio Maggiore
10. Zattere
11. Island of the Giudecca, Church of Redentore
12. Ospedale degli Incurabili
13. Gesuati Church
14. Church of Santa Maria della Visitazione
15. Campo di San Trovaso
16. Giudecca Island: Stucky mill
17. Church of San Sebastiano

From Accademia to the Salute to the Zattere

Gallery of the Accademia (tel. 5222247) Tuesday-Saturday 9.00 am-7.00 pm, Sunday and Monday 9.00 am-2.00 pm.
Basilica of Santa Maria della Salute (tel. 5230625). 9.00 am-12.00 am/3.00 pm-5.30 pm.
Church of Santa Maria della Visitazione (tel. 5224077) 8.30 am-12.30 am/3.00 pm-7.00 pm.
Church of San Trovaso (tel. 5222133) 10.00 am-5,30 pm, Sunday 3.00 pm-5.30 pm.
Church of San Sebastiano (tel.2750462) 10.00 am-5,30 pm, Sunday 3.00 pm-5.30 pm.
Length of visit
From Accademia to Salute: 2/3 hours
From Dogana to San Sebastiano: 2 hours.

Accademia
Zattere

BRIDGE ACCADEMÍA

The Accademia bridge was built in 1854. Until then the only way across the Grand Canal on foot was by the Rialto bridge. Get off the bridge and stop for a pause in Campo di Santa Maria della Carità.

CAMPO DI SANTA MARIA DELLA CARITÀ

There was a convent, a church and the old Scuola Grande di Santa Maria della Carità (now the home of the Accademia di Belle Arti e delle Gallerie) here.

The portal to the left of the museum entrance was the way in to the school.

Look for reliefs depicting the patron saints. On the left St. Leonard, protector of prisoners, is holding the links of a chain and on the right is St. Christopher, a sort of gentle giant who, without knowing it, carried Jesus across a river on his back.

Above is the Madonna receiving within her cloak the brothers of the school in their traditional habits. These works date back to 1377.

Look for this symbol, it is that of the Scuola Grande di Santa Maria della Carità. Now go into the courtyard. The old door you see on the right with the pointed arch and symbol was the entrance to the Scuola Grande.

The other sides of the courtyard belonged to a convent built during the second half of the XVI century by Andrea Palladio (1508-80), little of which is left now.

GALLERIE DELL'ACCADEMIA

The academy of painters and sculptors founded in 1750 stood near St. Mark's but in 1807 it was moved to the complex made up of the church, Scuola Grande di Santa Maria della Carità and XVI century monastery of the Lateran Canons. To make it easier for the young people studying art at the Academy it was decided to create spaces where paintings and sculptures could be exhibited.

When you have bought your ticket, go to the first floor.

You are in **room 1**, the **Chapter room** of the old Scuola Grande della Carità. It is very large because it had to accommodate meetings where all the brothers were present. Look at the XV century ceiling: it is coffered and the gilding is pure gold. In each panel there is a small angel with eight wings. God is in the centre and the prophets at the sides in the roundels of the ceiling.

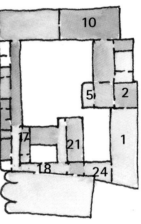

There are some paintings on wood dating back to the XIV century. In almost all of these the background is gold to represent the splendour of divine light. Look for a polyptych (a painting made up of several panels or folds) of the **Coronation of the Virgin**, by **Paolo Veneziano** (1320-62).

The centre panel shows Christ is crowning Mary. The two main figures are both seated on thrones, one opposite the other and at their feet are the sun and the moon, symbols of the passing of time and eternity.
Look at the figures represented. They are flattened onto the gold background. Mary is seated but her body seems to lack consistency, we could not rest anything on her knees, for example. Her face is stylised and a dark, unnatural colour.

In the same room is a **polyptych of the Annunciation** executed a few years later by Lorenzo Veneziano (who worked between 1356 and 1372). The background is still gilded but the figures are no longer static and immobile. Their positions are more natural and their bodies have acquired a greater consistency.

Now go into the **Albergo room (24)**, where the directors of the school would meet and the registers and most precious belongings were kept.

Take a look at the canvas above the door you came through.

It is the **Presentation of Mary at the Temple** and it was painted by Titian (Tiziano Vecellio, 1490-1576) especially to decorate the walls of this room. How is this easily understood?
1. because Titian painted stones arranged as though a window opened in the bottom right
2. because the colour of Mary's clothes is similar to that of the ceiling
3. because the steps that Mary is going up are the same as those in the room.

Go to **room 2** and look for the **St. Job altarpiece**, painted in around 1478 by **Giovanni Bellini** (1430-1516).

This is a very important work for several reasons: first of all for the first time the figures are represented all together and not separated by different frames; Bellini paints using very luminous colours that give volume to the bodies and depth to the painting; furthermore, for the first time in paintings of this type, perspective is used. It is a technique that allows the depth and thickness of objects and people to be conveyed in the same way as the eye sees them.

Bellini's painting was such a success that it became the model for future altarpieces.

Go on to **room 5**, where you will find the **Tempest** by Giorgione (1477-1510). The artist's life is still shrouded in mystery. He died young after executing a large number of works, but without signing any of them. He painted directly onto the canvas, without any

preparatory drawing, something only an incredibly talented person could do. The Tempest, painted between 1506 and 1508, was for a long time called "the gypsy and the soldier". What exactly the artist had wanted to represent had already been forgotten by the XVI century and still today the meaning it not clearly understood. Giorgione seems to have captured the moment before a summer storm breaks; on the right a young woman sits breastfeeding her child. Standing up, on the left, a soldier is watching

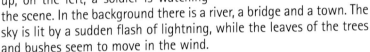

the scene. In the background there is a river, a bridge and a town. The sky is lit by a sudden flash of lightning, while the leaves of the trees and bushes seem to move in the wind.

Go to **room 10** which houses XVI century paintings.
Look for the work by **Jacopo Robusti called Tintoretto** (1515-94) of **St. Mark freeing a slave**.

The scene is very dramatic: the servant of a gentleman of Provence had gone, against the wishes of his master (on the right dressed in red), to pray over the body of St. Mark and had been condemned to death for his disobedience.

While the slave is lying on the ground and is about to be killed, St. Mark arrives almost in a nosedive from above, destroys the instruments of torture and saves the poor man.
The movements and the speed of the action are rendered by violent contrasts of light and shade.
Try observing the figure in the foreground, he is half lit and half in shadow, so that he seems to be turning to the right.

A whole wall in the same room is occupied by a single painting, the huge **Feast in the house of Levi**, a work by **Paolo Veronese** (1528-88).

In 1573 the Dominicans of Santi Giovanni e Paolo asked Veronese to paint a Last Supper. The artist painted for them what you are looking at now, using luminous, very bright colours. The Dominican fathers liked it a lot but the Inquisition (which governed over all religious matters) sent Veronese to trial for having included what they considered irreverent figures (the dwarf holding a parrot and soldiers dressed in German clothes) in a religious painting. Veronese argued that the artist must be free to create and invent as he pleases. In the end he was let off on the condition that he changed the offending figures. Well, he did not change the figures, he left the painting exactly as it was. He changed the title instead. The Last Supper became a dinner at a wealthy gentleman's house at which Jesus was a guest!

Go to **room 17** which contains pictures from the XVIII century. Look for a small painting by **Pietro Longhi** (1702-85) which captures moments from the lives of the nobility of the time: the **Concert** in which while three musicians are intent on playing their instruments, three men of the church, quite disinterested in the music, are playing cards; the **Dressmaker**, the moment when costly materials were to be chosen for new dresses. A small girl,

dressed like an adult, is giving a little dog a compass to sniff; in the **Dance lesson**, the teacher is showing a rather awkward lady some dance steps, under the attentive gaze of an older noblewoman.

Now look for two paintings by **Francesco Guardi** (1712-93), a famous eighteenth century view painter. It was not so important for Guardi to show places in Venice exactly as they were so much as to express the emotions these views aroused in him. In **View from the island of San Giorgio** the light seems to envelop everything: the water, the sky and the buildings. Look at the church on the island, it seems made of light and air.

Go to **room 21.** You will find the nine canvases painted by **Vittore Carpaccio** (1460-1526) between 1490 and 1500 for the school of Sant'Orsola. They tell the story of Ursula a Christian princess, daughter of a king of Britain.

(1) The kneeling ambassadors are bringing the king the marriage proposal of Hereus, son of the king of England. On the right is Ursula listing the conditions on which she will accept the marriage. She wants Hereus to become a Christian and to go with her on a pilgrimage to the Pope. (2) Her father Maurus gives her answer to the ambassadors and they (3) return to England. In the fourth picture (4) there are four scenes. Starting from the left look for: Hereus leaving England and saying goodbye to his father; in the centre Hereus meeting Ursula; in the following scene the betrothed greet king Maurus and his wife; finally, in the background the departure of Hereus and Ursula for Rome, followed by a train of eleven thousand maidens. (5) In the fifth

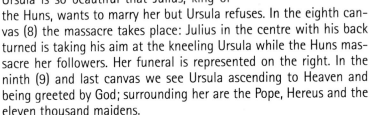

canvas we see an angel appearing to Ursula and announcing her martyrdom. The two continue on their way and arrive in Rome to visit the Pope (6) who greets them outside the walls of the city, as was the custom for important visitors.

In Cologne (7) though the Huns are waiting to kill Ursula, Hereus and the Pope. Ursula is so beautiful that Julius, king of the Huns, wants to marry her but Ursula refuses. In the eighth canvas (8) the massacre takes place: Julius in the centre with his back turned is taking his aim at the kneeling Ursula while the Huns massacre her followers. Her funeral is represented on the right. In the ninth (9) and last canvas we see Ursula ascending to Heaven and being greeted by God; surrounding her are the Pope, Hereus and the eleven thousand maidens.

Can you find the Pope?

To go out you have to return to corridor XVIII then go down the stairs on the left.

CAMPO SAN VIO

Leave the Gallery behind you and turn right, walking along beside the old Convent of the Carità. You will be in rio terrà Foscarini. It was once a canal that linked the Grand Canal to the Giudecca canal, but in 1863 it was filled in. Turn left into calle nuova di Sant'Agnese. Cross over the bridge and you are in campo San Vio (an abbreviation of the names of saints Vito and Modesto).

There was a church here — now demolished — and the palace of Bajamonte Tiepolo, who in 1310 had plotted against the Republic of Venice.

When the plotters were discovered the house was destroyed and it was decided to hold a grand feast at which the doge would be present, along with representatives of the government and the scuole Grandi. To make the arrival of the court from the Grand Canal more dignified, several houses were pulled down and the campo was extended as far as the canal.

Look for this detail

On the right there is a small chapel, nowadays a private house. It was built in 1865 on the site of the old church of San Vio. There is still a religious building in the campo though — the Protestant evangelical church dedicated to St. George. Over the portal you can see a relief of the saint battling with the dragon.

PALAZZO VENIER DEI LEONI

Carry on along the calle of the church and then along fondamenta Venier. Take calle di San Cristoforo on the right. You pass right beside palazzo Venier dei Leoni (of the lions).

The name refers to the fact that in the XVIII century the Venier family kept lions in a big cage in the garden.

Now the palace is the home of the Peggy Guggenheim Collection, one of the most important contemporary art museums in the world.

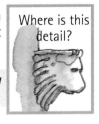

Where is this detail?

Continue along calle San Cristoforo and stop for a moment when you get to the bridge.

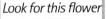

Look for this flower

CAMPIELLO BARBARO

When you have crossed the bridge you will be in campiello Barbaro, a characteristic place, very quiet and green. It appears in almost all films shot in Venice.

CA' DARIO

At the foot of the bridge on the left beyond the garden is Ca' Dario, a beautiful Renaissance palace with polychrome marble decorations.
It is said to bring bad luck to its owners though, all of whom have died mysterious or violent deaths.

Look up among the roofs for a strange wooden construction resting on small pilasters. It is a covered roof-terrace and is typically Venetian. You reach it either up a small staircase or through an attic.
As far back as the XV century the noblewomen of Venice used to go

up on these terraces wearing a "solàna" (a large hat without a crown through which they pulled their hair), a white dress and carrying a bottle with a strange potion in it and a sponge.
They spent hours wetting their hair and letting it dry in the sun to lighten it. In dialect the expression "la solàna" is still used to say that someone has had too much sun.

Go along calle Barbara and cross San Gregorio bridge. From here you suddenly see the large dome of the basilica of the Salute.

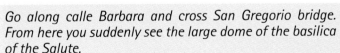

CAMPO SAN GREGORIO

Go along calle Bastiòn, on your left you will come to calle Traghetto, the gondola ride across the Grand Canal. It has been there for years and years. Continuing along the calle you come to campo San Gregorio.

The big building in front of you, nowadays a restoration laboratory, was the church of San Gregorio and the building on the left, a monastery. Go down calle de l'Abbazia.

The building above the portico, which leads to the wooden bridge, once linked the church to the monastery.

In 897 doge Pietro Tribuno (888-912) put a large iron chain that reached from here to Santa Maria del Giglio, the church at the end of the calle on the other side of the Grand Canal. This was to stop enemy ships from entering the city.

Cross over the bridge and you will get to the basilica of the Salute.

BASILICA OF SANTA MARIA DELLA SALUTE

In 1630 plague broke out in the city. It was devastating and very contagious. It was said to have started with a carpenter who lived nearby and went to work at San Clemente, an island in the lagoon. The ambassador of the duke of Mantua, who had fallen ill, was kept on the island in isolation. Soon the disease spread to Venice killing a great many people.

In October 1630, doge Nicolò Contarini (1630-31) made a vow to the Madonna: if the plague stopped, he would build a magnificent church dedicated to her. Shortly afterwards, the epidemic died down.

It was decided that the sanctuary should be placed in one of the most prestigious areas of the city, right in front of the basin of St. Mark.
On 1 April 1631, doge Contarini laid the foundation stone and, to celebrate the occasion, coins were minted with the image of the doge (who died the following day!) and these were put in a hole in the centre of the church.

The shape of the church had not however been decided yet. Something unique was needed, a building no one had ever seen before, and with lots of light. A competition was held.

La pianta della chiesa è:

1. round
2. rectangular
3. octagonal

The design that won was by a young architect called Baldassarre Longhena (1598-1682) and it was decidedly original in comparison with the traditional Venetian churches.

The exterior is white, in Istrian stone and it is covered by a dome. The entrance door, framed by four columns, is enormous and it is opened only on 21 November, the feast day of the Madonna della Salute.

Over a million stakes were used for the foundations of the church!

In 1687 it finally opened and doge Marcantonio Giustinian promised that in future the doge in office and his retinue would make an official visit to the church on 21 November each year, crossing the Grand Canal on a bridge made of boats.
The feast of the Salute is still one of the most important appointments on the calendar in Venice.

Look up and see if you can find some unusual coil shapes.
What are they for?
1. to allow people on the outside to hear what is being said in church
2. to show which way the wind is blowing
3. to help to support the weight of the dome.

Go up the steps, turn towards the basin of St. Mark. In the XVII century the buildings near the church were not so high.

The big white church must have been even more magnificent and imposing then, seeming as it did to rise up directly from the sea!

When you are inside, turn to the left and stop in front of the main door. You can see the main altar from here, just as the architect had planned. If you get the chance (it is usually only allowed on 21 November) go to the centre of the floor and look around: it is the only spot from which you can see all the altars at the same time.

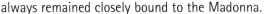
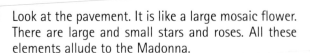
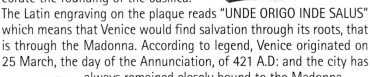

In the same point, in the centre of the octagon, there is a small bronze plaque beneath which in 1631 the doge placed the coins minted to celebrate the founding of the basilica.
The Latin engraving on the plaque reads "UNDE ORIGO INDE SALUS" which means that Venice would find salvation through its roots, that is through the Madonna. According to legend, Venice originated on 25 March, the day of the Annunciation, of 421 A.D: and the city has always remained closely bound to the Madonna.

Look at the pavement. It is like a large mosaic flower. There are large and small stars and roses. All these elements allude to the Madonna.

On the altar is a picture of the Madonna with a dark face. It is a XIII century Byzantine icon (a word that derives from Greek and means holy image) brought from Candia (Crete) by Francesco Morosini, an important Venetian admiral who was also doge between 1688 and 1694.

On 21 November — the feast of the Madonna of the Salute — the icon is adorned with jewels and is covered with gold. Only the faces of Mary and the angels remain uncovered.

Above the altar is a group of sculptures by Josse Le Court (1627-79).

The Madonna is in the centre, holding Jesus in her arms. She is turned towards Venice, represented by a noblewoman kneeling with her arms outstretched, who is offering thanks to the Madonna for ending the plague (the horn, the doge's headdress and symbol of the city, is meekly placed on the ground).

On the right is the plague, an ugly old witch-like woman with torn and crumpled clothes who is being chased away by an angel with a torch.
The plague seems to be about to lose her balance and fall down off the altar!

PUNTA DELLA DOGANA

With your back to the basilica of the Salute, turn right towards the basin of St. Mark. Where the fondamenta begins so does the punta della Dogana, the Customs point, a triangular tongue of land in the middle of the basin between St. Mark and the island of San Giorgio.

Since ancient times, the goods that arrived in Venice were unloaded and weighed at San Biagio, in the Castello zone.

By 1414 though, it was clear that one customs point was not sufficient for all the merchandise arriving in Venice.

Therefore, to check the goods arriving by sea and the ships stopping at St. Mark, the Sea Customs were created on the tip of the Salute, while at Rialto the Land Customs were established for merchandise arriving by land.

This area was for a long time also called Salt point because the salt supplies of the Republic were kept in storerooms here.

Look for two statues. They are supporting a golden ball on their backs. The ball represents the world, above which is the image of Fortune.

What was it for?

1. it was a target. Only those who managed to hit it could enter Venice
2. people watched the tides using a periscope from here
3. it was a weather vane to see which way the wind was blowing.

ISLAND OF SAN GIORGIO MAGGIORE

If you stop on the outermost part of the punta della Dogana, in front of you is the island of San Giorgio Maggiore and the façade of the church of the same name.

Once it was called the island of cypresses because there were so many cypress trees, orchards and vineyards there. There was also a salt mine and a windmill. In the X century there was a monastery that soon became rich and famous. The church of San Giorgio was built in 1566 by Andrea Palladio (1508-80), a famous architect who worked on other Venetian churches too. Look at the four large columns with a triangle above them: they remind us of the classical temples.

The novelty of this style of architecture was in fact the use of elements taken from classical temples for the decoration of religious buildings.

Every year, on 26 December, St. Stephen's day, the doge used to come here to attend a Mass, at which two choirs sang. The choir of St. Mark and that of the monks of the island's monastery. All the

other buildings you see on the island, including the one with the red plaster on the right, at one time belonged to the Benedictines. Now they are part of the Giorgio Cini Foundation, a study and cultural research centre for history, art and music.

FONDAMENTA DELLE ZATTERE

The fondamenta delle Zattere unwinds right along the Giudecca canal, from the punto della Dogana (Customs point) to San Basilio. This long waterside was built in XVI century to unload wood. The name "zattere", meaning rafts, refers to the way in which tree trunks were carried down the river Piave to the lagoon.

Departing from punto della Dogana, the far end of the Zattere, you come to the Sea Customs buildings, build in 1414. Walk along the fondamenta towards the Umiltà bridge.

Just before the bridge there is a building with a small observatory. How can you recognise it?

ZATTERE AI SALONI: THE SALT STORES

Continue along the Zattere, cross the Umiltà bridge and you will come to rio Terà dei Saloni.

The Zattere ai Saloni start here. "Saloni" refers to the large warehouses where salt was stored.

The constructions you see on the right (now used by the Canottieri Bucintoro who put their boats there before regattas) were the old salt deposits.

Salt, which Venice produced in great quantities thanks to the numerous salt mines in the surrounding areas, was the only raw material produced locally and it was one of the Republic's major sources of income.

The stores were built in XIV century and were then renovated over the centuries that followed.

THE ISLAND OF GIUDECCA

Go to Ca' Bala bridge. When you are at the top, stop a moment and look across to the other side of the Giudecca canal.

The island full of vegetation that you see on the left is the island of San Giorgio Maggiore, while directly in front of you is the island of Giudecca. The Giudecca is made up of 8 small islands. Some people think its name recalls the Jews of Venice who lived here in the XIII century. Another theory is that Giudecca derives from judegà, "the judged", a term used to describe the offspring of the noble Venetian families who were confined to the island after committing serious crimes. Subsequently, the Giudecca became a place for relaxation, where smart villas with beautiful gardens were built.

CHURCH OF THE REDENTORE

The large white church in front of you is the church of the Redentore. It was designed by Andrea Palladio (1508-80) and building began in 1577.

In 1576 the population of Venice was deci-mated by a terrible outbreak of the plague and the city's government made a vow to Christ: if the plague ceased, they would erect a mag-nificent church dedicated to the Redeemer. The plague did end; the site was chosen, easily visible from Piazza San Marco and Andrea Palladio was chosen to design it. As on all important occasions, coins were minted with the picture of the church on them. Then a large procession was held in which the doge, the Patriarch and all the most important dignitaries and representatives of the scuole Grandi took part. A bridge of boats stretched from the piazzetta of St. Mark to the Giudecca.

Still today on the third Sunday in July, the whole city takes part in the feast of the Redentore.

A bridge of boats is created that reaches from the Zattere to the island of the Giudecca, regattas are held, there are fireworks displays, people go out on boats and parties go on all night all over Venice.

Look at the façade of the Redentore church.

The architect seems to have put one church on top of another! It is rather reminiscent of a classical temple, with columns and two tympana, one over the entrance and one over the façade.

OSPEDALE DEGLI INCURABILI

If you keep on walking you will come to a long building; it is the hospital for incurable diseases.

It appears originally to have been for people with diseases from which they inevitably died. Later, when it became used for abandoned babies, the name was never changed.

In the hospitals the male children were taught a job, while the girls were instructed in music and singing.

Over the years the standards became higher and higher and their concerts were famous all over. The uniform of the girls in this hospital was turquoise.

Above each door you will see a head.

The first has a serious and rather sad expression and this was the door through which the "incurables" passed when they died.

The face over the other door is smiling and, of course, the people who got better passed through this one.

CALCINA BRIDGE

Cross over the bridge of the Incurabili, the next bridge you come to is the Calcina bridge.

Until about thirty years ago there was a swimming pool here.

In actual fact, there was a rectangular space of canal water, with walkways and changing rooms and a fence around it, where people went swimming. The water must have been a good deal cleaner than it is now!

Cross the Calcina bridge, then proceed along the fondamenta beside the Giudecca canal.

From the Calcina bridge onwards, the Zattere become very lively. Why?
1. it is a safe place with lots of light
2. you can buy the best gianduia chocolate ice creams in the city here
3. the view is breathtaking.

CHURCH OF THE GESUATI

Carry on and you will come to the large white façade of the Gesuati church on the right. Its real name is the church of Santa Maria del Rosario, but everyone calls it the Gesuati church, because of the fathers to whom it belonged. The church you see was built in the XVIII century, by which time the Gesuati (their order was suppressed in 1668) had actually been replaced by the Dominicans. In 1728, the Dominican fathers turned to Giorgio Massari, an able architect of the time, for a new project because the nearby church of the Visitation where they held their services had become too small to hold the congregation. The church was originally designed to have one side on the water and in fact to the right of the Gesuati church is rio terà Foscarini which was once a canal.

> Look for the arches under which the later filled-in canal passed.
> What was the name of the rio?
>
> --

The church has a single large nave.

Go in and look at the ceiling. It was frescoed by Giambattista Tiepolo (1696-1770) who completed the whole task in three weeks!

Tiepolo depicted space so that it seems to continue beyond the surface of the ceiling.
The figures seem to be moving away from us, sucked up into the sky.
Notice how steep the steps are!

CHURCH OF SANTA MARIA DELLA VISITAZIONE

When you leave the church, walk on a bit and you will come to Santa Maria della Visitazione.

The elegant façade belongs to the XVI century.

> Look for this face with its mouth open. What is it?
>
> 1. an old type of entry phone
> 2. one of the many holes spread around the city in which to drop notes revealing secrets
> 3. a sort of loudspeaker so that the Mass could be heard outside.

SQUERO DI SAN TROVASO

Walk along the Zattere as far as the San Trovaso bridge, turn right immediately before it, you will be in fondamenta Nani.

From here you can see the San Trovaso boat builders yard, one of the few establishments left of its kind. Boats and gondolas are still built and repaired here. The company was founded in the XVII century and it is still privately owned. The houses overlooking the yard are mostly made of wood and look as though they belong more to the mountains than to the city.

Why are these houses like the ones in the mountains?
1. families that started up boat building businesses or worked in them came from the Dolomites and so they built houses in a style that was already familiar to them
2. people who worked with wood built houses where it could be stored if necessary
3. people who made gondoliers did not like the style of Venetian houses.

CHURCH OF SAN TROVASO

Go along fondamenta Nani until you get to the bridge; cross over and turn left towrds the church of San Trovaso.

Go up to the entrance, walk past the bell tower and look for a large mask. It was to keep away the devil, who otherwise... would scare the people to death by ringing the bells whenever he wanted!

The church has two façades, one facing the campo and one facing the canal. Do they seem: THE SAME DIFFERENT

The campo di San Trovaso was on the border between two rival groups who lived on opposite sides of the city. The Nicolotti, who wore a beret and a black belt, and the Castellani, who also had a beret, but their belt was red. To avoid fights, each gang had its own entrance in church, one on the canal and one on the campo.

Go into the church and look for a painting of St. Chrysogonus, dressed in gold and riding a beautiful white horse. The sky is gold, the cloak, ribbons and horse's harness, all blowing in the wind, are decorated with enormous precision. He almost seems like a fairy tale knight.

CAMPO DI SAN TROVASO

When you leave, go to campo di San Trovaso.

Look carefully at the campo. It is about half a metre higher than the fondamenta. Beneath the well there was a cistern in which rain water was collected. When it was decided to increase the size of the cistern the entire paving of the campo had to be raised.

The name "San Trovaso" refers to:
1. the protector saint of gardening tools
2. a saint that helped to find lost items
3. Gervase and Protase twin brothers and saints.

SCUOLA DEI LUGANEGHERI

Leaving the campo behind you, cross the bridge, walk along calle del Magazen and under sottoportico Fioravante. You will get back to the Longo bridge on the Zattere. Turn right.

You will soon come to a two-storey building (at numbers 1473-1473/A) made of Istrian stone. It was once the school of the Luganegheri. This was the name given to the cold meat, lard and sausage workers. At the top in the centre is a statue of St. Anthony abbot, their patron saint. In the Middle Ages the monks devoted to him raised pigs because they thought the lard served to cure a type of herpes called, in Italian, Saint Anthony's fire.

STUCKY MILL

Now turn towards Giudecca island. The very large red brick building is the Stucky mill. The Stucky family were Swiss industrialists. In 1885 Giovanni, the real founder of the dynasty, commissioned a German architect to build a large industrial complex on the island of Giudecca, where the family business occupied nearly 200.000 cubic metres of space — a huge area!

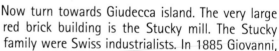

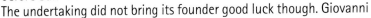

Ernst Wullekopf, as the architect was called, designed a building that resembled the style then in fashion in Northern Europe, but it did not suit Venetian taste at all. The Municipality only let him go through with it to avoid 200 workmen from being sacked.

The mill however became one of the largest and most modern factories in Europe. It produced and packaged flour and pasta using the most up to date technology. It was the first building in the city to have electric light, so the Giudecca was the first zone in Venice to be lit, even before San Marco.

The undertaking did not bring its founder good luck though. Giovanni Stucky, one of the wealthiest men in the city (he lived at Palazzo Grassi), art collector and one of the founders of the Biennale was murdered by a worker at Venice station.

The mill was active until 1954 and it is under restoration now.

CHURCH OF SAN SEBASTIANO

Go along the Zattere until you get to calle del Vento. Walk along it as far as San Basegio. Then go along fondamenta di San Sebastiano, then cross the bridge of the same name on the left. You will be at the church of San Sebastiano.

The church of San Sebastiano dates back to the XVI century.

The interior was decorated by a famous painter, Paolo Caliari, known as Veronese (1528-88). He loved to paint large figures, fake architecture from which people seemed to lean out, images that created an illusion of reality, using bright, luminous colours.
The subjects in this church are episodes taken from the Bible.

On the ceiling is the story of Esther, a beautiful young Jewish girl who brought an end to the persecutions of her people by marrying Assuero, king of Persia.
The moment in which Esther is crowned queen is represented in the centre.

1. Pugni bridge
2. Church of Carmini
3. Scuola Grande dei Carmini
4. Campo Santa Margherita
5. Scuola Grande di San Rocco
6. Basilica of Frari
7. Scuola Grande di San Giovanni Evangelista
8. Campo San Polo

From Pugni bridge to San Polo

Church of Carmini (tel. 5226553)
7.30 am-12.00 am / 3.00 pm-7.00 pm
Scuola Grande dei Carmini (tel. 5289429).
9.00 am-12.00 am / 3.00 pm-6.00 pm
Scuola Grande di San Rocco
(tel. 5234864) 9.00 am-5.30 pm
Basilica Santa Maria Gloriosa dei Frari
(tel. 2750462). 9.00 am-6.00 pm,
Sunday 1.00 pm-6.00 pm
**Scuola Grande di San Giovanni
Evangelista** (tel. 718234)
Sunday and Monday 10.00 am-4.00 pm
Church of San Polo (tel. 2750462) 10.00
am-5.30 pm, Sunday 3.00 pm-5.30 pm
Length of visit: half a day

 Ca' Rezzonico

THE PUGNI BRIDGE

Departing from campo San Barnaba, turn left; after a short walk along fondamenta Gerardini, you will come to the "Barca".

Have you ever seen a floating fruit and vegetable shop?

Go up the bridge of Pugni and stop.

> What is pictured low down at the corners?
> 1. a flower   2. a foot   3. an oar

In the past, until 1705, the citizens of Venice were divided into two different factions, the Castellani (those whose lived in the Castello, San Marco and Dorsoduro zones) and the Nicolotti (who lived in the Cannaregio, San Polo and Santa Croce areas). Clashes were frequent and often took place on the city's bridges. These fights, which at times involved hundreds of people, were not repressed or punished by the government, who merely decided the rules. The conflicts could only take place betwen September and Christmas and they followed a precise set of rules. Once the challenge had been made, referees were chosen, as was the bridge where the fight would take place. On the chosen day, each faction would arrive to a roll of drums and the sounding of trumpets and would present its champions who

either fought alone or in small groups.

The real "war" only began after this. It consisted of a gigantic free-for-all with hundreds of men battling to get to and claim the centre of the bridge.

Fisticuffs were allowed and, until 1574, sticks too. These were sharp double-edged reeds. In the fight, which lasted several hours, tens of people died. The picture you found on the bridge is the shape of a foot which marked the contestants' starting point.

CHURCH OF THE CARMINI

Leave the bridge and go along the rio terà Canal (an old canal that was later filled in), at the end of which you will find campo Santa Margherita on your left.

Continue along on the left until you reach the church of the Carmini. From here you can only see the side entrance, covered by a small roof erected in the XIV century.

At that time the buildings you see now did not exist and this side of the church could be seen easily from the campo. This is why the small portico was added and decorated with very old, XI-XIII century, moulds. These are all adorned with animals, each of which has a particular meaning in the Christian religion.

Try naming each picture.

1. two peacocks drinking at the fountain
2. a wading bird with a big fish in its mouth
3. an eagle pecking a hare's head
4. a griffin and a hare
5. an eagle and a hare
6. an eagle and a hare.

SCUOLA GRANDE DEI CARMINI

The Scuola Grande dei Carmini is opposite the side entrance of the church, on the corner to your right.

It was the last school in Venice to receive the title of Scuola Grande, in 1767. It was built in around 1669 after a design by Baldassarre Longhena (1598-1682). The upper room is frescoed by Giambattista Tiepolo (1696-1770), a famous painter who decorated churches, palaces and villas in colours that seemed to capture the sunlight.

CAMPO SANTA MARGHERITA

Now go back towards campo Santa Margherita via rio terà della Scoazzera (another canal filled in during the XIX century, along which there was a rubbish dump, in Venetian "'scoazzera").

Along the left side of the campo there are XIV century Gothic buildings. You can recognise them by their windows with pointed arches.

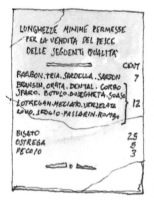

SCUOLA DEI VAROTERI

In the middle of the campo there is a building on its own which seems to have been put there by accident. This is the Scuola dei Varoteri, the school for skin tanners. It was built in 1725, an exact replica of the old one that had to be pulled down.

The relief you see high up of the Madonna receiving the brothers comes from the old building. In the bottom left, on the same side, there

is a plaque like the one at the Rialto that indicates the minimum size acceptable for the fish sold at the market. Every morning even today there is a small fish market here, except for Mondays because the fishermen stay at home on Sundays.

CHURCH OF SANTA MARGHERITA

Leave the campo and go towards the bridge of San Pantalon; shortly after entering the calle you will find the remains of a bell tower and the old church of Santa Margherita.

They have been recently restored and now house an auditorium of the university. According to legend one day a ferocious and hungry dragon saw a young girl and ate her up. The unfortunate dragon did not just eat any young girl though, it was St. Margaret and she used the cross she was holding in her hand at the time to open the dragon's stomach and climb out unscathed.

Look for a relief with St. Margaret and the dragon and at least 6 other monsters.

Cross the bridge of San Pantalon and go left. When you have passed the church, turn right immediately into campiello Angaran.

Look on the wall in front for this relief. What does it represent?

1. a gentleman who lived here
2. the owner of a textile factory that was once here
3. a XII century Byzantine emperor.

THE SCUOLA GRANDE DI SAN ROCCO

Retrace your steps and carry on down calle San Pantalon on the right; turn right at the end into crosera san Pantalon, then imediately to the left into calle dello Scaletèr. Go over the bridge and, from campiello San Rocco, go under the sottoportico of the same name; turn left and you will be in campo San Rocco.

The Scuola Grande di San Rocco which you see on the left, is one

of the six Scuole Grandi that have been in the city for centuries. It started in 1478 to help the poor and sick, especially during outbreaks of the plague.

San Rocco, or St. Rock (1296-1327), was born in France and spent his life looking after plague sufferers. It is said that during his stay in Piacenza he too became ill yet

managed to survive. However, when he returned home he was so thin and looked so terrible that nobody recognised him and he was imprisoned.

Only his faithful dog kept him company. This is why St. Rock is often represented with a small dog. In 1485 his body was moved to Venice and he became one of the protectors of the city.

His feast day is still celebrated on 16 August every year and the "tendon del doge", a sort of large canopy, is erected in the campo.

The Scuola di San Rocco was built between 1489 and 1549 but its present look is the result of alterations that have taken place over the years.

When the building was completed, the brothers launched a competition to find a painter to decorate the rooms. The participants had to submit a sketch (a rough outline of the general idea) of St. Rock ascending into heaven.

Jacopo Tintoretto (1518-94), a famous and extremely crafty Venetian painter managed to deceive everyone. He submitted a finished painting claiming that it was his way of making a sketch and, to cap it all, he gave the painting to the school as a present. Needless to say, he won the competition.

The interior is built like a typical school of its kind. On the ground floor is the large room where visitors and the needy were received. The upper floor was the Chapter room where the meetings of the brothers were held, and the Albergo room where the directors of the school used to meet.

Go into the entrance hall. Here Tintoretto painted scenes from the Gospels (1582-94).

Look for the **Rest on the flight into Egypt**, the painting that follows the **Nativity**. If you cover one of the two parts (either the figures or the landscape, which ever you want) with your hand, the painting still seems complete, as if two separate parts had been put together. It seems like a theatre scene. Go towards the end of the room and look for two paintings with female figures reading, at dusk and at night. They are St. Mary Magdalen and St. Mary the Egyptian. A magical light makes the landscape seem unreal. The trees lit by the moon and the sun seem almost like fireworks!

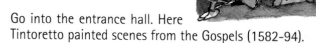

Go up the two flights of stairs, cross the Sala Grande and you will come to the Albergo room at the end on the left.

Look for an oval painting on the ceiling. It is the supposed "sketch" by Tintoretto. St. Rock and all the figures that surround him are looking at us from above, leaning out almost as though they were about to topple over on top of us. When they saw this painting the brothers gave Tintoretto all the other rooms to decorate. The job took him nearly twenty years.

The walls are decorated with scenes from the **Passion**. In front of you as you go in is the enormous painting of the Crucifixion. Christ is at the centre of the picture. The area of light behind the cross seems to underline the drama and solitude of Christ by separating him from the others.

Look for this gentleman: it is the artist himself.

Look too on the counter for a small painting of three apples. This piece of canvas was folded under a frame for years. The bright and lively colours are still the original ones. Since it was not exposed to the light, it has not changed as the other works have.

Return to the Chapter room (in which Tintortto worked from 1576 to 1581, while he was busy on other works, such as the Ducal Palace paintings). Here there are stories from the Old and New Testaments, which allude to the altruistic aims of the school, namely to cure the sick (in the middle of the ceiling is the bronze serpent that cures the Hebrews), give drink to the thirsty (on one side of the ceiling Moses is making water gush out from the mountain) and to feed the hungry (on the other side of the ceiling the collecting of the manna).

The wooden chairs set out around the room are decorated with caricatures and personifications sculpted by Francesco Pianta the Younger, an XVII century artist. Have a look for Tintoretto. To the left of the entrance to the large staircase there is a big parchment made of wood, on which the artist revealed the identities of the various personages and the meanings of the allegories.

BASILICA OF SANTA MARIA GLORIOSA DEI FRARI

After leaving the Scuola Grande di San Rocco, turn right. Immediately on the left in front of you is the apse of the very large church of Frari.

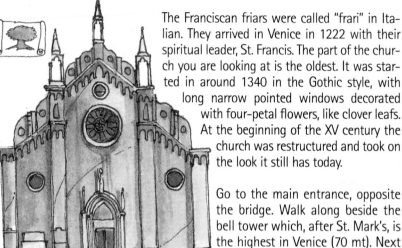

The Franciscan friars were called "frari" in Italian. They arrived in Venice in 1222 with their spiritual leader, St. Francis. The part of the church you are looking at is the oldest. It was started in around 1340 in the Gothic style, with long narrow pointed windows decorated with four-petal flowers, like clover leafs. At the beginning of the XV century the church was restructured and took on the look it still has today.

Go to the main entrance, opposite the bridge. Walk along beside the bell tower which, after St. Mark's, is the highest in Venice (70 mt). Next to the entrance door there are two rounded windows. There is a coat of arms with a lily on the frame of the one on the left, beside the lion of St. Mark. The lily is the symbol of Florence and inside the church there is a chapel dedicated to the Florentines, who were bankers and merchants.

Go into the church, which is one of the city's largest.

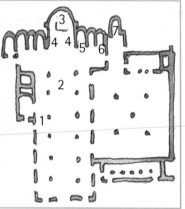

A number of important Venetians are buried here. These include doges, artists and condottieri.

Go up to the altar to the **right of the side entrance (1)**. It belonged to an important Venetian family, the Pesaro.
The painting on the altar, called the **Madonna di Ca' Pesaro** was executed by Titian (1490-1576), and it is a sort of family portrait.

The figures are arranged standing on steps; this is a completely new idea because Mary is usually shown in the centre with the saints surrounding her, and all the figures are usually on the same level.

> Who do you think the man on the left in the turban is?
> 1. after portraying the whole family, the painter decided to add the servants too
> 2. a Turk, symbol of Pesaro's victory over the people of Turkey
> 3. artists often included people from distant countries in their paintings.

Just think how boring it must have been to keep still while the artist painted you. In fact the child on the right has grown tired and has turned round. He seems to be looking at you.

Now go to the main altar. After a gilded arch on the right there is the **choir (2)**, where the brothers sat during the Mass. It belongs to the XV century, and is made up of wooden sculpted and carved seats, each with a different design. The last figure on the right near the bell tower is a portrait of the artist.

On the **main altar (3)** is a famous work by Titian of **Mary Ascending into Heaven**.

It is the most important painting in the church, some even say the most important in the whole of XVI century Venetian art.

When the friar who commissioned the painting saw it completed he did not want it, because it was too different from the style to which he was accustomed. Mary was like a real woman in flesh and blood, whereas she was usually represented as being of unearthly beauty.

Try imagining the painting divided horizontally into three parts (you can do it in the book, using a pencil):

a. in the lower section, the earthly area populated by man and his sentiments, are the astonished apostles, with their arms raised and faces turn heavenwards. Behind them the sky is blue;

b. in the middle section, the Madonna is in the centre, her feet resting on pillows of clouds, and all around her are cherubs. Here the sky is golden, lit by a warm light.

c. in the upper section, the divine part, where God is awaiting Mary with open arms. He is isolated within a golden light that represents His space, the sky where angels and saints are received into heaven. The luminosity increases as it nears God.

Along the walls of the **presbytery (4)**, where the main altar is, there are two very tall funeral monuments: these are the tombs of two doges, Nicolò Tron (1471-73) on the left and Francesco Foscari (1423-57) on the right.

Going towards the sacristy door, with your back to the main altar, you pass the small apse chapels on your left. These could be used by noble families or the confraternities who had to decorate them at their own expense. Stop at the first. This is the **chapel of the Florentines (5)**. On the altar is a statue **of St. John the Baptist**. It was sculpted in the XV century by the great Tuscan artist Donatello (1386-1466); it is the only work by him in Venice.

To decorate their chapels, the Florentines called an artist from their own city and in doing so they gave the Venetians the chance to see how they portrayed tension, tiredness and suffering. St. John, who had chosen to live in the desert, was pictured by Donatello with sunken eyes, thin cheeks and

an almost skeleton-like body. The Venetian artists would not have shown him like that because they preferred to make the figures softer, perhaps a little further from reality, but less tense, nervous and anxiety-filled.

Go to the sacristy door. If you look up you will see other funeral monuments. The equestrian statue (6) on the left is of Paolo Savelli, a commander who died of the plague in 1405. Does his horse remind you of other more famous ones? The sculptor most probably drew inspiration from the horses of St. Mark.

Go into the **sacristy (7)** — once it was the chapel of the Pesaro family — a look at the painting over the altar.

It was executed by Giovanni Bellini (1432-1516) in 1488: it is divided into three parts, but the saints and the Madonna are in the same room because there is only one floor.

The ceiling is very low either side and it seems almost as though the saints might hit their heads on it!

Notice the Madonna on the throne. The red wall behind her has been painted as though it were a real niche, with a real space behind the throne.

Instead it is all on the same plane, a flat board of wood, but Bellini manages to represent space and atmosphere by his use of colour and light.

If you should be in this church at Christmas, do not forget to look for the famous Nativity scene that is created in one of the chapels.

SCUOLA GRANDE DI SAN GIOVANNI EVANGELISTA

When you go out, cross the bridge opposite the portal of the church, turn left along fondamenta dei Frari, cross the San Stin bridge, go left along rio terà San Tomà, then turn right immediately into calle del Magazén. After a little way, you will come to the small campo of the Scuola on the left. This is where the Scuola Grande di San Giovanni Evangelista is, nowadays used for conferences, conventions, concerts, exhibitions. It is hard to visit.

Its symbol is the hook at the top of the bishop's crosier.

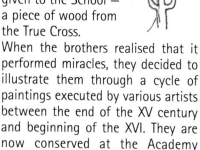

The School was founded in 1307. Sixty years later a precious relic was given to the School — a piece of wood from the True Cross.

When the brothers realised that it performed miracles, they decided to illustrate them through a cycle of paintings executed by various artists between the end of the XV century and beginning of the XVI. They are now conserved at the Academy Gallery and are known as the cycle of the Miracles of the Cross.

Why is there an eagle represented over the gate leading to the courtyard?

1. to frighten away the doves

2. it was the symbol of St. John the Evangelist

3. only those who could hit it with a crossbow on their first try could join the School.

CHURCH OF SAN POLO

Go back along calle del Magazén, then turn left into calle del Tabacco, cross campo San Stin and the bridge. Go on until you get to the Frari bridge. Do not cross over, but keeping it on your right, walk all the way along the fondamenta; turn left into rio Terrà, then left into calle seconda dei Saonèri (the street where the

soap makers worked), which will bring you to calle dei Saonèri. There turn left, cross the San Polo bridge and walk along the salizzada.

At the end on your left is the church of San Polo. The entrance has a Gothic portal made of different coloured marbles.

The building was altered on several occasions and it is a combination of different styles.

> Look for the bell tower. There are two lions at the bottom. What are they holding in their claws?
>
> 1. a dolphin and a flask of wine to give the passers by something to drink
> 2. a rope and a bag, symbol of wealth
> 3. a snake and the head of a doge, punished for treason.

CAMPO SAN POLO

Go to campo San Polo. Once a canal ran along beside the buildings on the right hand side of the campo, but it was filled in in the middle of the XVIII century. Here, in one of the largest campos in the city, markets and processions used to be held. During carnival time, parties, masked balls and even bull hunts took place as well!

On 26 February 1548, Lorenzo de' Medici, known as Lorezaccio, was killed here. He had murdered his cousin Alessandro de' Medici, who was on his way to becoming absolute ruler of the city of Florence.
However, Cosimo the other cousin, now a duke, found out that Lorenzo was hiding in Venice, and sent two hit men to kill him.

The Grand Canal, which the Venetians call the "Canalazzo", is shaped like a big S. It still follows the bed of a river that ran to the sea.
It divides the city into two parts, in each of which are three zones. It has been the main waterway for centuries.

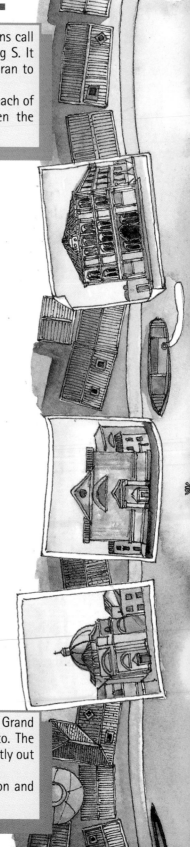

Ca' Vendramin Calergi

The palace built between the end of the XV century and beginning of the XVI is now the winter home of the Municipal Casino.
It was here that German composer Richard Wagner (1813-83) spent his last months and died.

Church of San Marcuola

It was designed by architect Giorgio Massari and built in the XVIII century, but the façade was never completed.
Its odd name comes from a combination of the names of saints Ermagora and Fortunato.

Church of San Geremia

It was built in the XVIII century; when the old church of Santa Lucia was demolished to build the railway station, the saint's relics were taken to San Geremia.

To see the palaces that overlook the Grand Canal, you have to take a vaporetto. The buildings almost invariably rise directly out of the water.
Either leave from Santa Lucia station and go to St. Mark or vice versa.

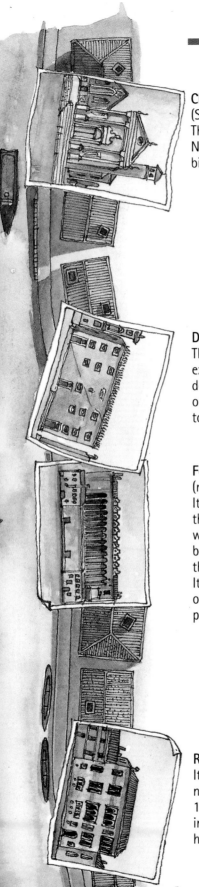

Church of San Stae
(St. Eustace in Venetian)
The church was built in the XVIII century. Nowadays it is used for concerts and exhibitions.

Deposito del Megio (millet deposit)
This was once the city's public granary. In exceptional circumstances, such as epidemics of the plague, the deposit was opened and the grain was distributed free to the hungry people.

Fondaco dei Turchi
(now the Natural History Museum)
It was built in 1250 as a private house in the style of the time: central open galleries with towers at either end. In 1621 it became the Fondaco dei Turchi, used by the Turkish merchants as their warehouse). It was rebuilt in the same way at the end of the XIX century because it was in very poor condition.

Riva di Biasio
It takes its name from a butcher by the name of Biagio who had a shop here in 1520. One day it was discovered that instead of selling pork, he was selling human flesh.... he was decapitated.

Rialto bridge

It was built at the end of the XVI century. Previously there had been a wooden bridge with a central part that opened to let pass the big boats that unloaded their merchandise along the Grand Canal.

Fontego dei Tedeschi

The building you see dates back to the XVI century, when the warehouse was rebuilt after a fire completely destroyed it. Here the German merchants deposited their goods and carried on their business. Nowadays it is the main Post Office.

Ca' d'Oro

This is the most beautiful and most famous Gothic palace in the city. Once the façade was painted black, light blue, white and above all gold. It was so splendid and so unlike the other buildings that it was remembered for its gold (oro) decoration, rather than for the name of its owner, Contarini. It is now the home of the Franchetti gallery.

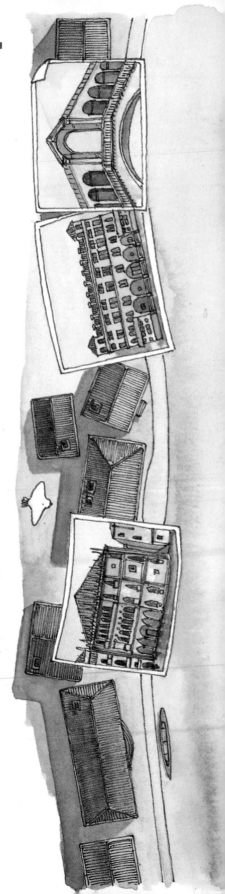

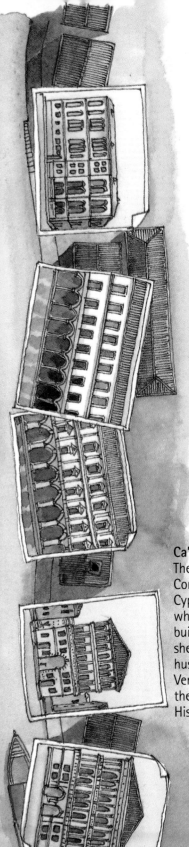

Palazzo dei Camerlenghi

The Camerlenghi were the three treasury magistrates, in charge of the Republic's finances.

The palace was built at the beginning of the XVI century; on the ground floor were the prisons where debtors and tax dodgers were held.

Fabbriche Vecchie

These were built in the XVI century and were the offices of the judiciary.

Fabbriche Nuove

These were built in the XVI century and were the offices for trade and commerce.

Ca' Corner della Regina

The name derives from its one time owners, the Cornaro (or Corner) and Catherine queen of Cyprus, who was born in 1454 on the site where three centuries later the palace was built. Catherine became queen of Cyprus when she married Giacomo III Lusignano, but on her husband's death she was forced to give up her Venetian properties. In exchange she was given the titles to Asolo. Ca' Corner is now where the Historic Archives of the Biennale are kept.

Ca' Pesaro (now the Museums of Modern Art and Eastern Art)

This imposing palace dates back to the XVII century.

If you have good eyesight or a pair of binoculars you can see the date of construction (in Roman numerals) on the sign held by one of the statues on the façade.

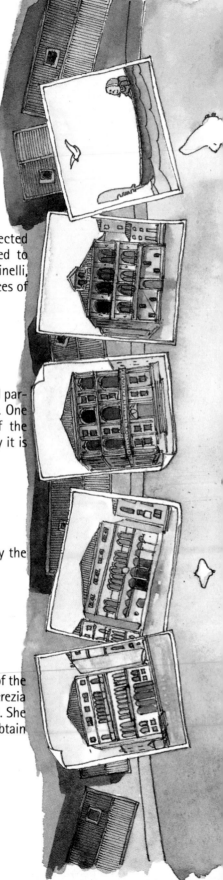

Ca' Corner Spinelli

This harmonious building was erected between 1400 and 1500. It belonged to the Corner family and then to the Spinelli, rich silk merchants. It is now the offices of a famous textile manufacturer.

Ca' Grimani

In the middle of the XVI century grand parties were held at this elegant palace. One of these was for the coronation of the Doge's wife Morosina Morosini. Today it is the Court of Appeal.

Ca' Farsetti

This XIII century palace was originally the home of a merchant.

Ca' Loredan

Another XIII century palace; it is one of the oldest buildings in the city. Elena Lucrezia Corner (circa 1620-84) was born here. She was the first woman in the world to obtain a university degree!

Details of the Canal:
- *it is 4 kilometres long*
- *it is between 30 and 70 metres wide*
- *its deepest point is 5 metres*
- *40 minor canals flow into it*
- *three bridges cross it*
- *between 1500 and 1600 18.619 windows overlooked it!*

Palazzo dei Dieci Savi
It dates back to the beginning of the XVI century. It was the seat of the ten magistrates who supervised taxes. Nowadays it is the Magistracy of the Waters.

Palazzo Grassi
It was the last great palace to be built on the Grand Canal. It belongs to the XVIII century and is now used for exhibitions and other cultural activities.

Ca' Moro Lin
It was constructed in the XVII century by uniting two Gothic buildings. The outcome was the "palace with the 13 windows".

Ca' Contarini of the figures
The name of this smart XVI century building derives from the family that built it and the two large white statues supporting the balcony.

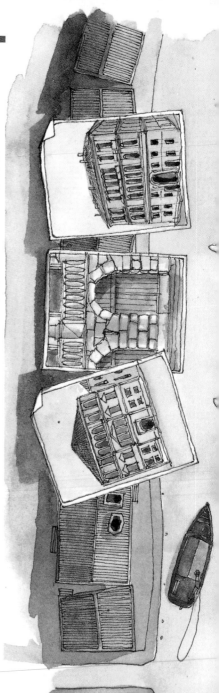

Ca' Rezzonico
Building began at the beginning of the XVII century and terminated the following century. Now it is the museum of Eighteenth century Venetian art.

Ca' Foscari
It dates back to the XV century. Now it is the home of the University. It is a magnificent example of the style known as "Flamboyant Gothic", with quatrefoil pointed arches and loggias. It was the home of a very important Venetian family.
Henry III of France was a guest at Ca' Foscari when he passed through Venice in 1574. The signoria would ask owners of the finest palaces to give hospitality to important personages when they were in the city.

Ca' Balbi
It is located in "volta del canal", which is where the canal curves round. It is the home of the Regional offices. You can see two pinnacles on the roof.

Ca' Pisani Moretta
This XV century palace has a strange second name which seems to derive from a corruption of Almorò (which then became Almoretto and subsequently Moretto), perhaps an ancestor of its owners. The interior has remained unchanged and it is used for grand parties and sometimes for filming.

Ca' Barbarigo dalla Terrazza
The palace takes its name from the magnificent terrace overlooking the Grand Canal.

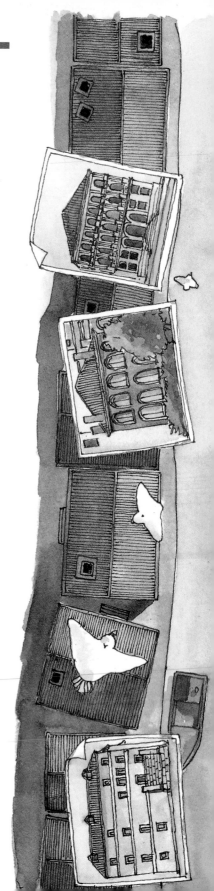

Palazzo Corner della Ca' Granda

It belonged to the Corner, or Cornaro, family, one of the most powerful in the city, who consequently lived in one of the grandest and most imposing palaces in Venice. Now it is the Prefecture.

Casina delle Rose o Casetta Rossa

It the XVIII century it was the studio of sculptor Antonio Canova.
Between 1915 and 1918 poet Gabriele d'Annunzio lived there. His mistress Eleonora Duse, who was very jealous, is said to have bought a house right opposite on the other side of the Grand Canal, so that she could keep an eye on him.

Ca' del Duca

This large building was begun in around the mid XV century. It was bought by Francesco Sforza, duke of Milan (from which it takes its name). Later it was confiscated by the Republic, but it was never finished. The famous XVI century painter Titian had his studio here.

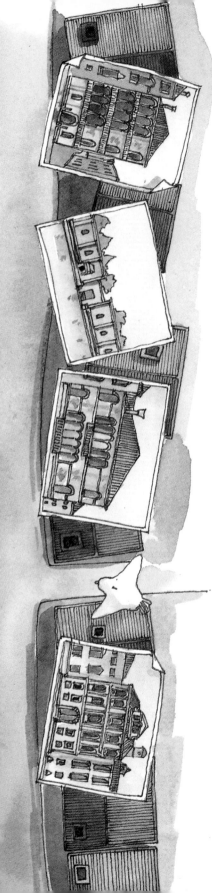

Ca' Dario

It was built at the end of the XV century, when the Dario family, who originated from Dalmatia, established themselves in Venice; the façade is decorated with multi-coloured marble, according to the fashion of the time.

Ca' Venier dei Leoni

It was commissioned by the Venier family in the XVIII century, perhaps to keep up with the Corner who had just built a splendid palace overlooking the Canal on the other side. It was never completed. Now it is the Guggenheim Foundation.

Ca' Barbarigo

It is famous for the XIX century mosaics on the façade.

Ca' Contarini degli Scrigni

Its name appears to derive from the caskets (scrigni) the family owned in its villa. In 1524 an excellent marriage took place in the basilica of St. Mark's followed by a banquet at the Ducal Palace. After the feast, the guests, bride and bridegroom were all escorted to palazzo Contarini by a procession of boats and accompanied by the firing of canons.

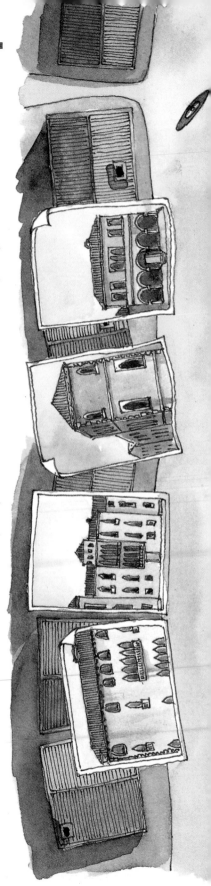

Palazzo Magistrato della Farina

The palace, built in the XVI century, was the seat of the Fontego della Farina magistrate; from 1756 to 1807 it was the Academy of painting and sculpture. Now it is the harbour master's office.

Ca' Giustinian

This is an old Gothic building which was turned into a hotel in the XIX century. Many famous people stayed there, including composer Giuseppe Verdi.

Ca' Contarini Fasan

This palace is also known as Desdemona's house. It is said to have been the home of Desdemona, unlucky wife of Othello, general of Cyprus, who killed her out of jealousy.
Shakespeare borrowed this famous story for his "Othello". The name "fasan" (pheasant), instead, would seem to come from a member of the family who was very fond of pheasant hunting!

Ca' Pisani Gritti

The exterior of this large XV century building was once entirely covered with frescoes. Nowadays it is a famous hotel.

Punta della Dogana

The Sea Customs is where, from 1414, the merchandise arriving by sea was unloaded and examined. The Land Customs are at the Rialto.

Basilica of the Salute

It was built in the XVII century to give thanks to the Madonna for ending a terrible outbreak of the plague.

Palazzetto Salviati

It is a recent building entirely covered in mosaics.

Murano
Torcello
Burano

MURANO
Church of Santi Maria e Donato (tel.
739056). 9.15 am–12 am/4.00 pm-7.00 pm
Glass museum (tel. 739586)
10.00 am-4.00 pm, closed Wednesdays

TORCELLO
Cathedral of Santa Maria Assunta (tel. 730084).
10.00 am-12.30 am/2.00 pm-6.30 pm
Church of Santa Fosca (tel. 730084)
10.00 am-12.30 am/2.00 pm-5.00 pm
Palazzo del Consiglio
(Estuary museum)
(Tel. 730761) 10.30 am-12.30 am/2.00 pm-
4.00 pm, closed Mondays and holidays.

For Murano:
Line 52 from piazzale Roma, Railway station, fondamenta
Nuove or San Zaccaria.

For Murano, Burano, Torcello:
Line 12 from fondamenta Nuove, Line 14 from San
Zaccaria.

MURANO: THE ISLAND OF GLASS

Murano is the largest island in the lagoon. It was already inhabited in Roman times. It was called Murano by the refugees from
Altino (an ancient city north-east of Venice on the mainland).
In the V century they fled here to escape the invasion of
the Huns. One of the gates of their city of origin was
called Morianos or Ammurianum.

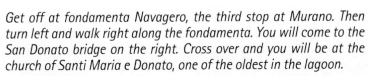

As time passed the port of the island
became an important landing stage for traffic in the Adriatic and
Murano became a lively trade centre; there were mills, salt mines
and hunting and fishing were both practised.

The island was always on excellent terms with Venice, which allowed
its administration a certain independence (until the fall of the

Republic). It was also permitted to
mint its own silver and gold coins
and medals, called "oselle".

In 1291 the glass furnaces were
moved here from Venice. Because
of the very high temperatures
there was always a risk of fires.

It was in this way that the island began to specialise in glass pro-
duction, so much so that before long it was the most important centre of its kind.

CHURCH OF SANTI MARIA E DONATO

*Get off at fondamenta Navagero, the third stop at Murano. Then
turn left and walk right along the fondamenta. You will come to the
San Donato bridge on the right. Cross over and you will be at the
church of Santi Maria e Donato, one of the oldest in the lagoon.*

It was built in the VII century and dedicated to Mary,
but in 1125 the body of St. Donatus was
brought here from the island of Cephalonia.
He was a warrior saint who had slain a dragon. After this, the church was dedicated
to him too.

In front of you is the apse, the most richly decorated part of the whole church. It was this area of the church you saw first when you arrived by sea, once the major means of access. The apse has niches, small columns, parapets and capitals made of Istrian stone and decorated with triangles, animals, flowers and crosses.

Either side of the entrance there are two ancient pilasters (I-II century A.D.) and above it a relief of St. Donatus with a disciple.

Go into the church. The building is divided into three aisles separated by columns of Greek marble, the capitals of which are all different from one another.

Now go and have a look at the façade overlooking the campo. It is:
1. very simple, made of brick with little marble
2. decorated with mosaics
3. all covered in strips of white marble.

The roof of the church is:
1. made of wood and like the bottom of a boat
2. made of stone and with a dome
3. flat, made of brick with three sky-lights.

On going in, stop in front of the entrance and look up above the arches of the columns for a wooden ball set into the wall. It is the so-called "bottazzo di Sant'Albano". This small cask, originally kept in the church of Burano together with the relics of the saint, is said to have filled miraculously with the wine used to celebrate the Eucharist. Since it was brought here in 1543 the miracle has never been repeated though.

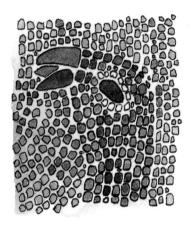

Look now at the marble mosaic floor and see if you can find a pattern with four big circles and a smaller one in the middle; there is a circular inscription that testifies to the fact that the present church was founded in 1141.

Incredible geometric patterns and numerous animals have been created in the mosaic: peacocks and griffins (the animals with wings and four paws) and between the columns, grasshoppers, eagles and cockerels.

Each has a symbolic meaning.

Try connecting each animal to the qualities attributed to it:

1. eagle   A. cunning
2. fox   G. immortality
3. peacock   R. power

Now put the letters corresponding to their qualities in order and look for the hidden word:

D   1   2   3   O   N

Go up to the main altar.
The remains of St. Donatus are kept in an urn here. Other bones, said to be those of the dragon, were brought from Cephalonia too.
See if you can find them near the saint. To tell the truth they are the bones of a whale.

The apse, where you are now, is decorated with a glass mosaic. Standing out against the large gold background is the Madonna in a light blue cape.

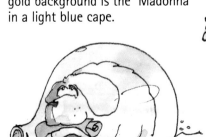

PALAZZO GIUSTINIAN

Go out of the church, back towards the bridge and carry on along to the right along fondamenta Marco Giustinian, palazzo Giustinian is at number 8.

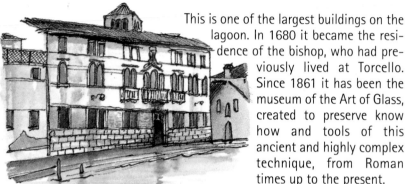

This is one of the largest buildings on the lagoon. In 1680 it became the residence of the bishop, who had previously lived at Torcello. Since 1861 it has been the museum of the Art of Glass, created to preserve know how and tools of this ancient and highly complex technique, from Roman times up to the present.

PALAZZO DA MULA

Continue along fondamenta Giustinian, which becomes riva Longa (or fondamenta Cavour) once you turn the corner. When you come to the Longo, or Vivarini bridge, start to cross over it.

From here, looking right, you get a good view of the Palazzo Da Mula, built between the XII and XIII centuries. It has a Gothic four-part window, moulds with animal designs and, in a niche above, a picture of the Madonna.

The palace was the country home of the noble Da Mula family who lived at San Vio in Venice.

The island of Murano was from the XV to the XVIII century a famous place for holidays, often reached by gondola. Here the Venetian upper class made their second homes, with magnificent orchards, vegetable gardens, vineyards and gardens. In the XIX century however, many of the buildings were knocked down and the mainland became more popular as a place for holidays.

FONDAMENTA DEI VETRAI

Go down off the bridge, turn left along the fondamenta dei Vetrai where almost all the furnaces were originally.
Today there is a long row of shops selling glass items. With the church of San Pietro Martire on your right, carry on straight along the fondamenta.

A little further on, before the Santa Chiara bridge, on the other side of the canal on fondamenta Manin, are the homes of the Obizzi and Sodeci (no. 6), with their porticoes directly on the water.

These are the typical glass blowers establishments-cum-houses.They were characteristic Medieval dwellings, in two parts, one on top of the other and clearly separate: in the upper part lived the owner of the factory, while the lower part contained the furnace, shop and storerooms.

At the end of the fondamenta you come to piazzetta Colonna. From here you can see Venice's cemetery on the island of San Michele, which is the other side of the Marrani canal.

You can go back to Venice from here.

Instead, if you want to go on to Burano and Torcello, you have to go to the "Faro" stop.

TORCELLO: THE MYSTERY ISLAND

Torcello is different from all the other islands. There are no houses, fondamenta, calli, campi, just canals and large uncultivated areas. It is the most evocative of the islands in the lagoon and its charm lies in the sense of mystery peculiar to abandoned places. It is hard to imagine that in the past it had some 10.000 inhabitants.

Torcello was perhaps already populated in Roman times. In the V century A.D. the inhabitants of Altino arrived here after fleeing the Huns. Once the danger had passed, many of them returned to their own city but two centuries later, under pressure form the Longobards, they returned to the island and settled here. They brought with them the relics of the first bishop of Altino, St. Elidorus, who became protector of the island. Also belonging to this period is the construction of the basilica of Santa Maria Assunta. In the X century Torcello was one of the most important islands in the lagoon; it was independent from an administrative point of view and could count on several highly productive activities (salt mines and a flourishing wool industry).
In the XIV century though

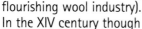

The name Torcello derives from:
1. a small tower in Altino
2. a musical instrument invented on the island
3. the torches that burned day and night on the island.

the course of two rivers was changed and many areas became swampy and malaria (a disease then common to swampy places) forced large numbers of inhabitants to move to nearby Venice. In 1680 even the bishop moved his see to Murano and little by little the island became almost deserted. Today it has only about thirty inhabitants.

DIAVOLO BRIDGE

When you get off the vaporetto, go along the fondamenta on the right, walking beside the canal.

As in Venice and Murano, there were buildings, churches, mills and even a few villas here too. Now there is nothing left, except for two bridges. The first is known as the "Devil's bridge" because it is said to have been built overnight by the devil himself!

1. it is an ordinary bridge and there is nothing odd about it	T	F
2. all bridges were built like this once	T	F
3. children were thrown from the top of the bridge into the water, so that they would learn to swim	T	F
4. fist fights were held on it	T	F

THE CENTRE OF THE ISLAND

Carry on along the fondamenta, with the bridge to your right until you get to the island's second bridge. You will find yourself in an open space, at the end of which is a small square.

PALAZZO DELL'ARCHIVIO AND PALAZZO DEL CONSIGLIO

These two small Gothic buildings in front of the churches are the only evidence of the grandeur that was.
The building with a portico and Gothic window with three lights was the Archives, where documents were kept.
The small construction beside it, with a small campanile and external Gothic staircase, was once the Council building.
Today both are occupied by the Estuary Museum which conserves valuable remains that have come to light during excavation work.

ATTILA'S THRONE

Look for the so-called throne of Attila, king of the Huns. In actual fact Attila does not appear to have anything to do with this marble seat, which was instead for the bishop or whoever represented political power.

CATHEDRAL OF SANTA MARIA ASSUNTA

With your back to the throne, look at the cathedral of Santa Maria Assunta and church of Santa Fosca. Walk to the cathedral and go in. Eighteen columns divide the space into three aisles. At the end of the nave there is a kind of gate, known as the iconostasis. It served to separate the area occupied by the congregation from that where the Mass was celebrated.

Between the small columns, at the bottom, in the reliefs of the large panels are lions and peacocks. The lion is the symbol of strength and the water the peacock is drinking is a symbol of the grace of God.

On the other side of the iconostasis is the choir. Look on the left for a marble slab with a long Latin inscription which indicates the date of the founding of the church; it dates back to 639 A.D. and it is the oldest document written about Venetian history. The half dome above the main altar has a mosaic executed between the XII and XIII centuries. It shows Mary holding Jesus in her arms. Look at what she is holding in her left hand: it is a handkerchief to symbolise all the tears she will shed for the death of her son. The mosaic is known as the "Mater dolorosa". At the foot of the Madonna are the 12 apostles and beneath the window is a picture of St. Elidorus, whose body is kept beneath the main altar.

Behind the altar, at the top of the brick steps, was once the throne where the bishop sat on important occasions. Look at the level of the apse; it is slightly higher than the rest of the church. This is because below it is the crypt, which is reached from the side aisles. The floor of the church is made of coloured marble pieces, laid out to form a geometric pattern.

Why was the floor not made of pieces of glass?

1. glass would have reflected the light and blinded the congregation
2. the floor would have been too slippery
3. marble is more resistant.

On your way out, observe the huge mosaic above the door: it represents the Last Judgement. It belongs to the XII century, and was made by the same mosaic workers who decorated St. Mark's. The story reads from top to bottom.

CHURCH OF SANTA FOSCA

When you leave the church, walk along the portico on the left and go into the church of Santa Fosca. It was built between 1000 and 1100.

It is a simple construction made of brick. The exterior is an octagon surrounded by a portico, while the inside has a Greek cross plan (with four equal arms).

Originally this was not a church but a martyrium, a place where the remains of a martyr were kept and venerated. Inside you can see the bodies of St. Fosca and Maura. The roof is made of wood. A dome may have been planned but it was never built, perhaps because they were afraid the walls would not support it.

If you wish to, you can visit the bell tower too. There is a fantastic view.

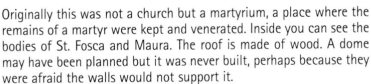

BURANO: THE ISLAND OF LACE

The island was probably inhabited already in Roman times and in the V century the refugees from Altino settled here. They called it Boreana in memory of a gate in their city of origin, so called because it was exposed to the bora wind.
Burano was always considered less important than Torcello and nearby Mazzorbo, but in the XVI century when the lace industry flourished it made a considerable contribution to

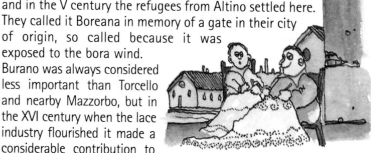

the Republic's economy. Furthermore, thanks to its being far away from stagnant waters and protected from the wind, it was never subjected to malaria or other diseases typical of swampy areas (unlike Torcello). Nowadays there are about 4.000 inhabitants.

VIA BALDASSARRE GALUPPI

From the pier of the vaporetto, walk along via Andriana Marcello. When you are in fondamenta San Mauro, among the lace shops, turn left. With a stone bridge on your right, walk towards a wooden bridge. Cross over and you are in via Baldassarre Galuppi.

It takes its name from the musician born on the island and consequently known as il Buranello. Look around. The houses are all alike, on two floors, separated from one another only by their bright colours of red, green, light blue, purple.

Why are the houses so brightly coloured?
1. to keep mosquitoes away
2. there was a competition held once a year. The house with the most beautiful colours won
3. the women used to paint them, so that the husbands recognised them from afar when they returned from their fishing trips.

PIAZZA GALUPPI

Walk to the end of the road, then turn left into piazza Galuppi.

Several Gothic buildings dating from the XIV century overlook the square. The first on the left is the palace of the Podestà. Today it is the museum and school of lace, for which Burano is famous.
Also typical of the island are bussolài. If you do not know what they are, go into a bakery, buy a packet and try them, they are delicious!

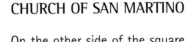

CHURCH OF SAN MARTINO

On the other side of the square is the church of San Martino, built in the XVI century.

Observe the façade — there is no entrance door.

Go in and look for the painting that tells this story. One day, the island's fishermen saw a large stone chest (among the nets). They tried to pull it up but were unable to do so. Some children who had watched what was going on decided to try to get it themselves and, to the amazement of everyone else, they succeeded.

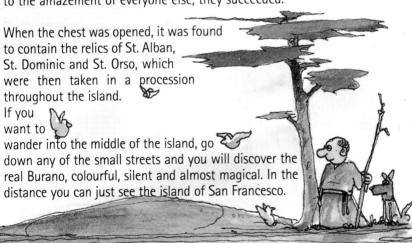

When the chest was opened, it was found to contain the relics of St. Alban, St. Dominic and St. Orso, which were then taken in a procession throughout the island.
If you want to wander into the middle of the island, go down any of the small streets and you will discover the real Burano, colourful, silent and almost magical. In the distance you can just see the island of San Francesco.

USEFUL INFORMATION

The Venice area code is 041.

For tourist information:
APTVE, Venice tourist bureau
Castello 4421, tel. 5298711
Piazza San Marco 2, tel. 5226356
Piazza San Marco 71/C, tel. 5208964
Santa Lucia station, tel. 719078
E-mail: aptve@provincia.venezia.it
www.provincia.venezia.it/aptve

MUSEUMS
In addition to those in the guide, with a little extra time you can also visit:

Ca' d'Oro Galleria Franchetti (tel. 5238790)
Cannaregio 3932. Open from 9.00 am to 2.00 pm
The Ca' d'Oro contains the baron Franchetti art collection. In the picture gallery you will find works by Mantegna, Carpaccio, Giorgione, Titian and Guardi.

Peggy Guggenheim Collection (tel. 5206288)
Dorsoduro 701. Open from 11.00 am to 18.00 pm. Closed Tuesdays.
One of the most famous contemporary art collections in the world; it was founded by the multi-millionaire American Peggy Guggenheim, wife of painter Max Ernst.

Archaeological museum (tel. 5225978)
St. Mark's square n. 52. Open from 10.00 am to 2.00 pm.
Important collection of ancient art: Assyro-Babylonian, Egyptian, Etruscan and Graeco-Roman finds which range from Neolithic to the early Middle-Ages.

Correr museum (tel. 5225625)
St. Mark's square n. 52. Open from 9.00 am to 5.00 pm; open until 7.00 pm from 1 April to 31 October.
It's the museum of Venice's history and culture. There are a lot of sections; the painting section is especially worth a visit.

Museum of Eighteenth century Venice (re-opens in 2000)
tel. 5204036
Dorsoduro 3136. Opening hours to be decided.
A collection of pictures, ceramics, hangings and furnishings set in surroundings with frescoed walls and ceilings evoke Venetian society of the eighteenth century, a time of splendour and decadence.

Naval History Museum (tel. 5200276)
Dockyard 2148. Open from 8.45 am to 1.30 pm. Until 1.00 pm on
Saturday. From 1.30 pm to 5.00 pm on Thursdays. Closed Sundays.
Venetian history at sea through models of ships, uniforms,
weapons, standards and war mementoes.

Museum of the Querini Stampaglia foundation (tel. 2711411)
Castello 4778. Open from 10.00 am to 1.00 pm and from 3.00 pm
to 6 pm. Until 10.00 pm on Fridays and Saturdays. Closed Mondays.
It houses miscellaneous objects and works (furnishings, porcelains,
weapons and other items); the picture gallery contains pictures by
Venetian artists from the XIV to the XV century.
Particularly interesting is the cycle of pictures by Gabriel Bella that
portray Venetian life in the XVIII century: ceremonies, games,
receptions and feasts.

HOLIDAYS
«In Venice you have a good time, you row and you go about in a
boat all year round».
Read here and you will see it is all true!

January: Regatta of the Befana
On 6 January the first regatta of the year is held: all the participant
are dressed like witches!

February: Carnival
It's a Venetian celebration that attracts tourists and curious people
from all over the world.
It takes place from 6 to 16 February. All calles and campos fill up
with processions of masks; games, concerts and shows take place
all the time.

May: Vogalonga
The marathon of regattas: it is 30 kilometres long!
Hundreds of crafts participate.

Ascension, holiday of the Sensa
It's a very old holiday that usually takes place on the second
Sunday of May. It was established after an important naval victory
in the year 998. Formerly the Doge travelled on the Bucintoro (a
sumptuous regatta boat all painted in gold) to the Lido where he
used to throw into the lagoon a ring saying «We marry you, Venice,
as a sign of true and ever-lasting dominion». All Venetians love this
holiday and they celebrate it with great solemnity.

June: Holiday of San Pietro di Castello

It's held during the last week of June. This holiday is restricted to the Castello zone, so not as famous as the other ones, but very entertaining with markets, stalls, puppets, competitions and games.

July: Holiday of the Redeemer

On the third Sunday of the month, every year since 1576 Venetians celebrate the end of a plague epidemic: the Giudecca canal and the St. Mark dock fill up with gaily decorated boats, while the faithful cross a specially built bridge of boats in procession towards the church of the Redeemer, on the Giudecca. At the evening, fireworks sparkle on the water of the lagoon.

September: Historic Regatta

It's the most important regatta in Venice: it is held on the first Sunday of the month. It begins with a historic procession that recalls the arrival in Venice in 1489 of Caterina Cornaro, queen of Cyprus. The procession is followed by competitions, first for women, then the very young, and finally the champions.

November: Madonna della Salute

In 1630 the basilica della Salute was erected to thank the Madonna for the end of a plague epidemic and the doge promised that every year he and his successors would visit the church by solemn procession,across a bridge of boats. Today the entire city still celebrates this feast day.

SOLUTIONS TO GAMES

Page 17	1/no; 2/no; 3/yes; 4/no; 5/no; 6/no; 7/yes; 8/yes.
Page 19	The correct answer is number 2.
Page 21	The correct answer is number 2.
Page 28	The correct answers are 1 and 2.
Page 33	The correct answer is number 1.
Page 35	The olive tree, symbol of peace.
Page 39	1st game: the correct answer is number 1.
	2nd game:the correct answer is number 3.
Page 42	The correct answer is number 2.
Page 43	1: the ceiling ones fall more naturally.
	2: the ones on the ceiling are more real.
	3: flat.
Page 44	The correct answer is number 1.
Page 45	St. George killing the dragon.
Page 46	Here are the 8 mistakes and the correspondent solutions:
	still young/old; crocodile/lion; dog/lion; tail/paw; castle/monastery; right/left; table/tree trunk; parrot/dog.

Page 47   1st game: Missing words: warrior, dragon, sword, princess.
2nd game: The dragon has: bat wings, snake's tail, dog's head, dog's hind paws, bird of prey's forepaws
3rd game: The different elements are: snout, ears, wings, tail.

Page 54   1st game: The correct answer is number 2
2nd game: 1. ruga, 2. calle, 3. campo.

Page 57   The false names are 3.4.5.

Page 59   Fallow deer.

Page 60   The square and the star do not exist.

Page 63   Detail of the hand of an angel holding a cello; it is in the centre opposite the saint.

Page 64   They're in the relief low down on the left. They are watching the Baptism of Jesus.

Page 65   The correct answer is number 2.

Page 67   The correct answer is number 1.

Page 71   1st game: the correct answer is number 1.
2nd game: the correct answer is number 3.

Page 72   The correct answer is number 1.

Page 73   The correct answer is number 3.

Page 77   1st game. A/ Detail of the canvas with the Adoration of the golden calf; B/ detail of the Last Judgement; C/ the intruder.
2nd game: the correct answer is number 1.

Page 82   The correct answer is number 1.

Page 87   The lion's head is on the corner between fondamenta Venier and calle San Cristoforo.

Page 89   The correct answer is number 3.

Page 90   The correct answer is number 3.

Page 92-   The correct answer is number 3.

Page 97   All three answers are correct.

Page 98   st game: Rio Foscarini.
2nd game: The correct answer is number 2.

Page 99   1st game: The correct answer is number 1.
2nd game: They're the same.

Page 100   The correct answer is number 3.

Page 104   The correct answer is number 2.

Page 105   1/D; 2/E, 3/A; 4/B; 5/C; 6/F.

Page 107   The correct answer is number 3.

Page 111   The correct answer is number 2.

Page 114   The correct answer is number 2.

Page 115   The correct answer is number 3.

Page 130   1st game: The correct answer is number 1
2nd game: The correct answer is number 1

Page 131   1/R; 2/A; 3/G. As a result you have the word: DRAGON.

Page 134   The correct answer is number 1

Page 135   The correct answer is number 2

Page 137   The correct answer is number 3

Page 138   The correct answer is number 3